My eyes wandered around the room, taking in the strange collection of humanity seeking to claim me as a fellow sufferer. If variety is the spice of life, this crowd was the jambalaya of affliction. Ted, sitting directly across the room from me, looked like he was taking a break from the Senior Tour: expensive pink sweater, silver hair, nice tan, Belgian loafers. Next to him, Rodney and Ruby looked as though they'd stepped out of the pages of *I'm a Biker and I Kill People* magazine. Matching leather vests were adorned with dozens of little pins, no doubt memorializing some of their more notable crimes. They also sported patches with the mysterious circle/triangle thingy on their matching biker chaps . . .

. . . Buck was retired military, and Pete was a cop . . . I knew that Julie was an assistant district attorney because she'd prosecuted most of my friends' DUIs. She smiled at me. Probably had a concealed carry . . .

Bored with people-watching, I tuned into some of what was being said. The topic was gratitude, and boy, was this hapless collection of human misery full of it! They were grateful that "the obsession to drink" had been lifted, that their "defects" had been removed (a work in progress for some, I could see), that they were conquering fears, returning to health, banishing resentment, saving family life, and filling up bank accounts. The list was endless . . . I looked around for the Kool-Aid and checked my watch.

—*From chapter 1*

Undrunk

A Skeptic's Guide to AA

A. J. Adams

Foreword by Mel B.

HazelDeN®

Hazelden
Center City, Minnesota 55012
hazelden.org

Library of Congress Cataloging-in-Publication Data

Adams, A. J., 1950–
  Undrunk : a skeptic's guide to AA / A.J. Adams; foreword by Mel B.
     p.   cm.
  Includes bibliographical references.
  ISBN 978-1-59285-720-3 (softcover)
  1. Alcoholics Anonymous   2. Alcoholics—Rehabilitation.   3. Recovering alcoholics—Services for.   4. Twelve-step programs.   I. Title.
  HV5278.A33 2009
  616.86'106—dc22

                                                        2008054850

Editor's note

The names, details, and circumstances may have been changed to protect the privacy of those mentioned in this publication.

This publication is not intended as a substitute for the advice of health care professionals.

Alcoholics Anonymous, AA, the Big Book, and the *AA Grapevine* are registered trademarks of AA World Services, Inc.

Unless otherwise noted, all quotations from *Alcoholics Anonymous* (the Big Book) are from the fourth edition, published in 2001 by AA World Services, Inc.

13 12 11 10 09   1 2 3 4 5 6

Cover design by Percolator
Interior design and typesetting by BookMobile Design and Publishing Services, Minneapolis

For Anita

I walked out of the fog and there you were—waiting for me.

Contents

Foreword by Mel B.   ix

Acknowledgments   xiii

Introduction   1

Chapter 1: A.J. Gets to an AA Meeting   5

Chapter 2: Getting It Wrong and Starting Over   17

Chapter 3: Why AA?   23

Chapter 4: Some AA Basics   45

Chapter 5: The Twelve Steps and Twelve Traditions   65

Chapter 6: Spin Dry:
            An Insider's Guide to AA Lingo and Slogans   97

Chapter 7: One-Year Progress Report   161

Chapter 8: Other People   175

Afterword   193

The Twelve Steps of Alcoholics Anomymous   195

Some Recommended Readings   197

About the Author   201

Foreword

There's a saying in Alcoholics Anonymous that nobody is too dumb to follow the Twelve Step program, but some alcoholics are too smart. Writing as an AA member with more than fifty-eight years of continuous sobriety, I can say that I've met my share of people who have dismissed the program because of such unexamined biases—and their lives have not always ended well.

A. J. Adams showed signs of being such a person when he attended his first AA meetings—and he continued to drink. Along the way, however, he began to understand that AA was quietly changing lives that had been all but lost. He studied and accepted the program and found his life miraculously changing for the better in only one year. The experience was so remarkable that he wrote this book to explain what he had found in AA that gave him continued sobriety and a completely new approach to life.

While AA is often described as a simple program, A.J. goes behind the scenes to show that AA has real depth and to highlight how and why it works. By writing in a personal, friendly style laced with a wicked sense of humor, he makes it easy to digest some of the deeper principles that have given AA its lasting power.

Who should read this book? It is certainly aimed at people who think they have drinking problems but are skeptical about AA or are resisting going to a meeting. (I don't know many people who *gladly* attended their first meeting!)

In addition, this book can be a good read for nonalcoholics who want to learn more about AA—especially if they think someone they care about has an alcohol or other drug problem—and how it developed from a chance meeting of two drunks in 1935. And since there have been a number of recent books, articles, and Web sites critical of AA, it's gratifying to have an advocate like A.J. who can lay out sound reasons why AA is still working well, not the least of which being that it saved his life and the lives of millions of others.

I think you will find yourself being pulled in to A.J.'s story with the very first chapter. His first AA meeting in a shabby room in a rundown section of town was the kind of meeting that could be found anywhere in America. But, because he wasn't ready to accept the program and continued drinking until alcohol was, as he puts it, "moving in for the kill," this meeting could have turned him permanently away from the fellowship. Almost against his will, though, he picked up a few good ideas about AA and got the message that he should "keep coming back."

His real recovery started when the pain became excruciating, he lost his job (a common occurrence among unrecovered alcoholics and addicts), and his home life became terribly bleak and miserable. Prodded into rehab and humbled by defeat, he made a new beginning that worked this time. It is a story I've heard hundreds of times in AA, and A.J. gives it new twists that will carry you along.

One of the unwritten rules of AA is that one should utilize the program rather than analyze it, because too much analysis is said to lead to paralysis. I don't think this warning applies to A.J.'s discussion of what the AA program is and how and why it works, because it comes straight from the heart with no lecturing or proselytizing. Reviewing the history and development of AA, he concludes that AA's early years are a fascinating tale of serendipity and remarkable spiritual intervention. You'll also find him acknowledging the old-fashioned Yankee virtues that AA cofounders Bill W. and Dr. Bob picked up in their Vermont backgrounds. And if you're having trouble understanding the spirituality of the AA program, you'll get some help from his take on the subject in chapter 3. He sees spirituality as its own reward, as a source of energy to face life with confidence.

Beyond that, you'll find A.J. covering almost all of the AA basics in these pages: get a sponsor, attend meetings regularly, help yourself by helping others. You will even learn AA jargon and sayings that have evolved in the fellowship over the years. As he writes about all these topics, they seem to have fresh meaning for me, though I've heard them for years.

When you reach A.J.'s one-year progress report near the end of the book, I think you'll feel, as I do, that he has earned the happiness and success that his AA journey has brought into his life. This book is not only a great introduction to AA for people who are looking for something more than the "party line." It can also serve as a good reminder for newcomers—and even oldtimers like me—of what we need to be thinking, feeling, saying, and doing to stay on the right track as we trudge AA's Road of Happy Destiny.

Mel B.
Toledo, Ohio
Author of *New Wine, Walk in Dry
Places,* and other Hazelden books

Acknowledgments

Thanks first to "Swede" Hanson and Dennis Fitzgerald for the inspiration and encouragement that helped me through the writing phase of this project. The incomparable Judy Cleary showed me how to turn my manuscript into a book that might actually be published. Sid Farrar, at Hazelden, believed in *Undrunk* from the beginning and is the person who ultimately brought it into print. Special thanks to my two favorite English majors, Alec and Evan, who enthusiastically read and critiqued every word.

Introduction

*"Look, A.J., you can either keep on doing what you're doing
and continue to watch your life unravel, or you can give AA
a try and take a shot at a better life than you ever imagined.
What do you say?"*

Hmmm. Well, I'm going to have to think about that.

This was a real conversation. A year ago, I actually believed
that AA would just have to wait while I considered my options.
It was as though someone threw me a life preserver from the
Titanic, but I wasn't sure I wanted it because it was orange.

Alcoholics Anonymous (AA) has more than 2 million
members in 100,000 groups scattered across 150 countries.
No one who knows anything about alcoholism will deny that
the AA method is the single most effective treatment available for alcoholism. Yet millions of alcoholics still suffer poor
health and ruined lives—and some die—while the AA solution hides in plain sight.

At the end of an astonishing first year in AA that trans-
formed my troubled life into a daily joy, I asked myself why
so many alcoholics walk past AA. It's not as though AA is
only for a certain demographic. We are men and women;

old, young, and middlers; struggling to well-off; educated and not; straight and gay; all races; all religions, no religion; introverts, extroverts, pessimists, optimists, realists, skeptics, fools, cynics, and saints. We have one thing in common: we are alcoholics. Untreated, alcoholism gets worse and ultimately can kill us. AA offered a solution and we took it. I haven't met anyone in AA who invested sweat equity in the program and regretted it. Not a single person, and that's remarkable.

So why is AA the most effective treatment for alcoholism in the world and still ignored by millions? I think many who take a pass on AA do so for one of four reasons.

The first is the most obvious. They haven't suffered enough. Think of this as market economics. While the price of a fifth of vodka was $8.50, I was willing to pay. When it went up to $12.50, I didn't blink an eye. When the price started to include some friends and co-workers, I still paid. Hard to believe, but when it cost my reputation, I was still buying. It wasn't until I was asked to hand over my family, my health, and my self-esteem that I finally decided I couldn't afford a fifth of vodka.

A second reason for ignoring AA is that it seems old-fashioned. Picture this: a few desperate men get together in the 1930s to self-treat their hopeless alcoholism with a combination of what looked like voodoo therapy, Masonic solidarity, and do-gooderism. Until I saw the results with my own eyes, I was skeptical too. In twenty-first century America, we're used to having a pill delivered by someone in a white coat. AA is nothing like that. In fact, it's so homey it can invite ridicule from the casual observer. Until

I gave it an honest try, AA seemed quaint and a little peculiar to me.

The third reason AA puts some people off is that it seems too difficult. There's an AA saying that the program is "simple but not easy." But it's not that hard either. If it were, I wouldn't have stuck with it. What AA does is appeal to our better selves, which takes some getting used to for a lot of us. First, we have to be honest, and that can pinch in the beginning. Also, we have to have an open mind. Without it, we'll second-guess the program to death in a week. Humility is probably the hardest angel to summon. Like most alcoholics, I was anything but humble. Finally, recovery takes commitment. But most alcoholics do find the strength they need, especially if they've paid a visit to the gates of hell first, as most of us have.

The fourth reason why so many suffering alcoholics fail to embrace AA is also the reason I wrote this book: people either don't know anything about AA or they don't like what they think they know.

Getting to that first meeting can be tough.

I never made it into my first AA meeting. I set out for the appointed place in plenty of time, but I didn't realize that AA meetings can be deviously hidden. They're not hidden on purpose, but many are located in cheap, out-of-the-way commercial spaces and don't have big "Drunks Welcome" signs outside. I pulled up late in front of the meeting hall. I looked through the plate-glass window and saw about twenty people sitting in a circle. The meeting was obviously under way and I didn't know the AA etiquette for tardiness, so I drove to my local saloon to think it over.

The truth, of course, is that I was scared of AA and intimidated by the challenge of getting sober. What I knew about AA was a toxic mix of misinformation, misunderstanding, and caricature. I believed that only down-and-outers ended up in AA, and that the program was a kind of penance for past sins to which unlucky alcoholics were sentenced. None of that is true, but I encourage you to come to your own conclusions about AA, its program, and its people.

I hope this book makes it easier for others than it was for me to get to an AA meeting and stick around long enough to get the message. This two-step process is how most alcoholics *get AA*. Defeating our obsession with alcohol is only the beginning. AA is a fabulous lifestyle, philosophy, and personal code. That is what I mean by living *undrunk*.

CHAPTER 1

A.J. Gets to an AA Meeting

Alcoholics Anonymous.

Even the name put me off. Who'd want to be called an alcoholic, and why the secret-society thing? But I was on my way to a meeting for real this time, whether I wanted to go or not. My wife and kids were on my case about drinking, and I'd started to have a few at work that didn't go unnoticed. Although I dreaded it, I'd known for a while that I'd have to go to some AA meetings to take the heat off. I was running out of takers on my promises to cut back, so I was going to Plan B. I figured if I put in some time at AA, I could throttle my drinking back to a reasonable level and all would be well. Still, I felt a little queasy as I headed toward the address I'd gotten on the Internet.

As I drove through the November chill and the early evening gloom, I wondered why they couldn't put these things in places people could find. The meetings all seemed to be in church basements or out-of-the-way spots in rundown parts of town. And the meeting names—oh, the names: "Seaside Serenity," "Fresh Start," "Don't Worry, Be Happy." Why not just call it "Loserville"?

I turned into a slightly shabby strip mall that seemed to correspond to the address I had. Nothing looked like a meeting to me. Then I noticed some cars and bikes in front of one storefront. As I got closer, I counted a half dozen very nice motorcycles and a surprising collection of up-market sedans. There were some real junkers there too. It was an odd mix. I parked as far away as possible, so that anyone who might drive by and recognize my car wouldn't associate me with this sad affair.

As I walked toward the storefront, I scanned for a sign. Nothing. But what would an AA meeting sign say? After all, they're supposed to be anonymous. For some reason that seemed very funny, which I attributed to nerves and missing my 5:00 p.m. pint of vodka. A few of what I feared were my new friends were on the sidewalk, braving the cold to catch a smoke. "Is this the meeting?" I almost whispered, not wanting to breach anyone's secret existence. A couple heads nodded toward the door. I was afraid I'd stumbled onto the hearing-impaired meeting. "How come no sign?" I asked. The group chatterbox pointed to a circle with a triangle inside it, inscribed with the words "Recovery," "Unity," and "Service." Apparently this was supposed to mean something to everyone in the world. "Cool," I said and moved on.

I walked into the meeting room, which at least was warm. A few people looked my way with a combination of civility and curiosity. There was a fair amount of chat going on around me among the twenty-five or so people who seemed to know each other well. Laughter bubbled here and there around the room. In my increasing nervousness, I couldn't accept that anything humorous was going on here, and I wondered what moved any of these desperate people to laugh. No one had spoken to me yet, and the silence triggered a familiar

anxiety reaction. I really should have had a couple before trying this out. I was just about to pull out my cell phone to look
busy when I noticed a sign on the wall that read "Please place
cell phones in silent, vibrate, or stun mode."

I desperately needed something to do besides standing
there and feeling way out of my comfort zone. My eyes settled on the only exception to the 1950s classroom decor: a
world-class coffee bar. They probably didn't call it a coffee
bar here, but I knew how to pour myself a cup of coffee, so I
headed over. At last someone spoke to me. A smiley guy said,
"Leaded or unleaded?"

Knowing that the right response would be essential to
sustaining this budding conversation, I said, "Huh?"

"With caffeine or without?" smiley guy said.

"Oh," I mumbled, "I like the real thing."

"You're in the right place," he said, "and I don't just mean
the coffee." With a Santa-worthy wink, he poured my coffee
and moved on to another person.

With my coffee prop in hand, I took in the surroundings.
The room was dominated by a large conference table that had
seen many conferences. The surrounding chairs gave "ga-
rage sale" a bad name. The meeting leader's place was piled
with tattered books—the holy texts, I guessed. On the wall
were two large posters with the Twelve Steps and Twelve
Traditions; the language seemed stilted and archaic. World
War I–vintage slogans contributed to the funky feel of the
place: One Day at a Time. Live and Let Live. Easy Does It. A
trio of prayers, also on the wall, addressed the serious business of beating death by liver failure.

Desperate but no fool, I started inching toward the door

to make my escape. I nodded jovially at the people along the way and made little toasting motions with my coffee cup. But I'd missed my chance. Suddenly it was 5:30, and everyone was sitting down. As I considered just bolting, smiley guy from the coffee bar appeared out of nowhere: "Have a seat," he said. "I'm Tim." I surrendered but obstinately did not tell Tim my own name. I checked the wall clock against my wristwatch. I would be out the door at 6:30 on the dot. I started composing the line I'd call over my shoulder as I left, about an important meeting or a rookie babysitter.

My escape planning was interrupted by the leader's voice. "I'm Quincy, and I'm an alcoholic."

"Hi, Quincy!" the group responded with smarmy cheer.

"This is an open meeting of Alcoholics Anonymous. Our purpose is to bring the message of AA to the alcoholic who still suffers and to share our experience, strength, and hope with one another. Please limit your sharing to three or four minutes [*No problem for me,* I thought.] and let your language reflect the quality of your sobriety. Children are welcome, but we ask parents to remove them if they become disruptive. Please place your cell phones in silent, vibrate, or stun mode." The last comment occasioned a volley of polite laughter, as though no one had been reading it on the wall for the past hundred years.

The chair beamed at his loving audience and continued: "I've asked Deb to read 'How It Works,' but before she does, is anyone here for the first time or for the first time since their last drink? If so, I have a desire chip for you."

Absolute terror squeezed my heart into a walnut and sucked my lungs empty. A hundred eyes and fifty warm smiles focused on me. They wanted me to step up and accept what I could now see was a bright red poker chip. I screwed up my courage, took a deep breath, and ... did nothing. Well, not exactly nothing. I took a sip of coffee, looked around at no one in particular, and made my little toasting motion.

After what seemed like a really long silence, Quincy moved on: "Okay, let's go around the room and introduce ourselves." Oh, shit! This was really turning into a nightmare. I didn't even like this corny introduction thing at work meetings where I knew everyone. My get-up-and-run instinct switched back on, and I could feel my throat getting dry and tight. As my mind raced through possible escape plans, the introductions and hi's moved inexorably toward me. "I'm Judy, and I'm an alcoholic." "Hi, Judy!" "My name is Walter, and I'm a grateful recovering alcoholic." "Hi, Walter!" "Jake, alcoholic." "Hi, Jake!"

Smiley guy next to me announced that he was Tim and, amazingly, an alcoholic. Instead of saying "Hi, Tim" with the other ebullient greeters, I just stared at him for what seemed like a full minute and probably was. When I unwound my neck into the forward-looking position, I saw a picture of benign expectation that scared the shit out of me. Every face seemed to be wishing me enough courage to say my name. The pressure was excruciating.

I didn't recognize the croaking voice that said, "A.J., alcoholic." I expected a gasp of relief from the assembled, but the howdy train chugged on past me without a hitch. I had survived my first AA crisis. In fact, I had done pretty well—I hadn't blurted out my last name. Tim leaned over and whispered, "Good to have you here. Keep coming back."

I smiled my first real smile. I was going to be able to work this room after all!

Deb began to read "How It Works" from what I thought the chair called the "Blue Book" (it was blue). It was actually the Big Book, *Alcoholics Anonymous:* AA's version of received wisdom and truth. I settled in to listen for the remainder of my hour of penance. I thought it was funny that a secret society would blurt out its main secrets this way, but it was probably all crapola, so what did it matter?

My eyes wandered around the room, taking in the strange collection of humanity seeking to claim me as a fellow sufferer. If variety is the spice of life, this crowd was the jambalaya of affliction. Ted, sitting directly across the room from me, looked like he was taking a break from the Senior Tour: expensive pink sweater, silver hair, nice tan, Belgian loafers. Next to him, Rodney and Ruby looked as though they'd stepped out of the pages of *I'm a Biker and I Kill People* magazine. Matching leather vests were adorned with dozens of little pins, no doubt memorializing some of their more notable crimes. They also sported patches with the mysterious circle/triangle thingy on their matching biker chaps.

I could tell that Zack was a real estate agent, mainly because his polo shirt had the name of a real estate company stitched on the pocket. Miranda and Mary Ann were in their twenties. They sat together with infant carriers at their feet. Mandy was a fifty-something blond with a remarkably svelte body crammed into a miniskirt business suit fashioned from a blend of spandex and snakeskin. She kept leaving the room to answer her cell phone. Feeling my confidence and terrific sense of humor returning, I whispered to Tim, "She must be a bookie."

"Doctor," he replied, with that same annoying smile.

The mix of people was pretty remarkable. Buck was retired military, and Pete was a cop. I knew David owned the Ford dealership, because I'd seen him on late-night TV commercials. I knew that Julie was an assistant district attorney because she'd prosecuted most of my friends' DUIs. She smiled at me. Probably had a concealed carry. My favorite was Leon, who topped a five-day growth of beard and a mouth nostalgic for bygone teeth with a jaunty beret. He opened his sharing with excellent advice for us all: "AA is not about showing up, looking good, and sounding smart."

Bored with people-watching, I tuned into some of what was being said. The topic was gratitude, and boy, was this hapless collection of human misery full of it! They were grateful that "the obsession to drink" had been lifted, that their "defects" had been removed (a work in progress for some, I could see), that they were conquering fears, returning to health, banishing resentment, saving family life, and filling up bank accounts. The list was endless. The showstopper for me was the woman who said with a straight face that she was grateful for being an alcoholic, because the AA program apparently bestows on those willing to "work it" an idyllic life. I looked around for the Kool-Aid and checked my watch.

The centerpiece of a lot of the sharing seemed to be some reference to a "Higher Power." This was clearly code for God. In fact, the Big Guy was mentioned specifically by some speakers, but it was usually "God as you understand him" or something like that. If you were in a buying mood, you would apparently get a hell of a deal on God in AA. But this was a very personal universal architect—God in street clothes.

People talked about their God like a fishing buddy or a girl-friend from the gym. And the results? Whoa! You would not believe! According to my new friends, God would clean up your messy life, tell you what to do with it, help you do it, and make you feel great about it. All you had to do in return was "work the Steps" and "do the next right thing." This was called "spirituality" and was not to be confused with "religion." Beret guy told us that "Religion is for people who are afraid of going to hell. Spirituality is for people who have already been there." Actually, I sort of liked that.

In fact, I liked a fair amount of what I heard, despite my frantic desire to move the clock hands to 6:30. People spoke with astonishing candor about what had brought them to AA and what was going on in their lives now. The stories could not have been made up. For example, one guy's wife caught him cheating and ran over him with a golf cart. When he came out of the coma nine weeks later, he acknowledged that it was probably time for AA. The loss of spouses, children, and friends because of drinking was common. Wrecked careers, money trouble, and brushes with the law were popular too. There was also some terrific humor, considering the dark subject matter. Buck, the retired military guy, was recounting all the good things that happened to him after he got sober. He ended with ". . . and I lost 140 pounds." In the silence that followed, he added, "My ex-wife weighed 120."

The floor was being passed from one speaker to another through a game of "tag." Since no one knew me, I wasn't worried about being called on to speak. And even if I was, I'd noticed that a few people passed, saying something like "I think I'll just listen tonight." I'd forgotten about smiley guy, whose sharing did not inspire me to listen, until I heard my name: "I'd like to call on our newcomer, A.J." I could have killed him. It's amazing how fast the human heartbeat can go from 60 to 160. I forced my lips into a smile that surely looked more like a grimace and somehow thanked Tim for the opportunity to spill my guts in front of a bunch of strangers. I was terrified and had no idea what to say.

"I'm a newcomer, and I really appreciate the warm welcome I've gotten here tonight. I'm not sure that I'm an alcoholic— probably I'm not one. But I did want to come here and see what AA is all about. This has been a great evening. You are all so honest and frank. And I really appreciated the humor. The humor was really good and funny. I never did anything too bad when I was drinking except a couple one-car accidents, which can happen to anyone. Not that I'm judging any of you for the bad stuff you've done. That's all in the past and none of my business. Also, I just want to say that the coffee is great. It's better coffee than in the Navy. I was never in the Navy, but I respect any of you who were in the Navy, or in any part of the military. Thanks for letting me speak. One last thing: I'd like to donate some coffee since this was such a rewarding experience."

Fortunately, my terror had reduced the oxygen flow to my brain and I was unable to hear most of what I said. When I finished, everyone in the room offered the AA ovation: "Thanks, A.J."

I spent the last fifteen minutes of the meeting like a crazed zombie, smiling at everyone. Further toasting seemed over the top. The collection basket (they just call it "the basket") came around toward the end and I noticed that most people tossed in a buck, so I fished around for a single. I had actually stopped looking at the clock when Quincy announced that the meeting was over and asked a very troubled-looking young woman dressed in black and named Evangeline to "take us out." I hoped she was not armed. Everyone stood and took the hands of the people on either side. I hated this kind of stuff and had a hard time figuring out whether my hand should be offered in the under or over position. All went quiet and Evangeline said simply, "God."

The group then recited the Serenity Prayer, the original version of which is attributed to the American theologian Reinhold Niebuhr (1892–1971) and has become AA's signature devotion:

> God, grant me the serenity to accept the things I cannot change, the courage to change the things I can, and the wisdom to know the difference.

At that point, everyone (still holding hands) raised and lowered their hands rhythmically, chanting, "Keep coming back. It works if you work it." My hands were released by the hostage-takers on either side, and people started moving toward the door.

It was 6:30 on the button and I was full of joy. I had made it through my first AA meeting, and I was heading home to tell my wife that serenity and healing were at hand. I had seen the light and the way. Our problems would soon be over. "I'll drink to that," I muttered to myself.

I headed for the exit only to find my way blocked by smiley guy Tim. What the hell did he want? "Great to have you here, A.J. Here's a Big Book and a phone list of AAs who are available to talk anytime you feel the need. You'll like the book. It's a little stiff because it was written in the 1930s, but the message is profound. The first part describes what AA is all about. The rest of the book is stories about folks who've been helped by AA." I took my party favors and thanked Tim with my best attempt at sincerity. After all, I was sincerely glad to be leaving and could hardly wait to swing by the liquor store to secure a celebratory pint. As I turned for the door, Tim grabbed my arm gently but firmly and looked at me without the smile: "Keep coming back."

CHAPTER 2

Getting It Wrong
and Starting Over

I did keep coming back for a few months. I was getting decent mileage from my status as an AA member at home and on the job, where I shamelessly paraded my budding self-knowledge and remorse. Most important, going to AA meetings allowed me to keep drinking, although I vowed that I was cutting back as the AA magic worked itself in my life. I had always been somewhat of a secret drinker; now I was the 007 of drunks. I had pints of vodka hidden everywhere and had made disposing of the empties a science. In a way, I actually enjoyed the thrill of the new game.

At AA meetings, I continued to sling the bullshit. I saw myself as earnest and convincing, although as it turned out, no one else did. Even my most ridiculous bloviations earned me a heartfelt "keep coming back" or two. Hard to believe, but no one ever called me out as a fraud. Maybe I was amusing, but I doubt it.

The problem was that the game I was playing was no game. Alcohol was moving in for the kill, and I was getting dangerously close to becoming a statistic. After a few moderation failures, a one-car wreck, and scenes at the office and at home, I gave up on the AA facade and just drank. The end came quickly.

What tipped the balance? There is good medical evidence that alcoholism is a progressive disease. At the end, it progressed at a dizzying speed for me. Even though I was the one doing the drinking, I saw myself as the victim—of my wife, my boss, the doctor and shrink who were trying to help me, even my own children, who were frightened by what I had become and tried to avoid me. I was increasingly afraid of my unpredictability. I was so toxic that whenever my blood alcohol level dropped down anywhere near normal, I felt as though I was going to have a heart attack. My memories of this period are sketchy.

After a few months of this final spiral, I found myself in county detox on a Friday and in rehab two days later. My reaction to being in rehab was towering anger. Fortunately, my wife did not cave in to my demands to come home. After some early rebellion, including being late for everything and grinding on the nurses for more Librium, something strange started to happen. It began to dawn on me that "beating" rehab would be the emptiest of victories. I had spent years retreating from sobriety. Every time I felt the pressure to get straight, I made a concession or two—like cutting down or even going on the wagon for a while—and then went back to drinking as usual. In the military, they call this "defense in depth." You keep dropping back to what you hope will be a more defensible position, but you are still retreating. When I finally walked into an AA meeting, I wasn't there to quit drinking. I was there to *keep* drinking. After a few days in rehab, it started to sink in that this wasn't going to be my ticket to a few more months of drinking; it was probably my last chance to quit. That thought really scared me, so I ignored it.

As I look back, I think three things had to happen to give me a second chance. First, I had to understand that vital parts of my life were coming unglued. I had to feel genuine pain. I was not yet a shipwreck, but the trend lines were unmistakable. Second, I had to accept that my problem was alcohol. It was not this person or that one. It was not this unfair situation or that missed opportunity. It was booze. Third, I had to accept that I could not moderate my drinking. Every first drink led to a bunch more, no matter how good my intentions. I had to understand that getting this monkey off my back was not something I could do on my own.

After a week or so—and in spite of myself—I started to listen. Other people were clearly beginning to get it, and I wanted to get it too. They say that "AA moves at the speed of pain," and my pain in those first days was increasing as I realized that this might be my last opportunity to save my ass. The next part is either spooky or magical. I'm not sure exactly why, but my mind opened a crack to what was being said, and my listening turned to hearing. Months later I would understand that what came over me was *willingness*. Willingness to accept my alcoholism. Willingness to accept help. Willingness to work the recovery program. Willingness to save my own life. I have to admit, this really made everything that followed a lot easier.

Fast forward: I came out of rehab a month later with some basic tools to stay sober and get my life back into shape. I went back to my old AA group with only a vague memory of who I had been during the three months I'd attended while still drinking. I was scared, but instead of the hairy eyeball, I was greeted like a returning hero. Before long, I realized how many of my fellow AAs had also taken months or even years to start getting the program. Smiley guy Tim said, "Being an asshole and a fake in the beginning just makes you a stronger member in the end." I decided to buy that.

I connected with a great guy who was willing to "sponsor" me, which among other things means mentoring me through the Twelve Steps. I listened in meetings, read about AA, and told myself that others had done this and so could I. My life started getting better and happier almost immediately, and the improvements have been rolling in ever since. I don't miss drinking, but neither do I tempt fate with the notion that I'm now "okay." Worries that friends and associates would pity or avoid me were mostly unfounded. Because I was the last to realize how far gone I was, my alcoholism was no secret. Most people were happy for me, and more than a few confided that they or someone they cared about might want to give AA a try. Best of all, my wife and children are much relieved, proud of the work I've done, and grateful for the changes in me.

I left some wreckage in my wake, but AA has helped me set many things right and make amends where I could. Of course, some things and people simply had to be left behind. I was eased out of my job, and some friends who were really only drinking buddies disappeared from my life. Years of selfish drinking are bound to carry a price, but I obviously had it easier than the AAs who lost everything along the way or never recovered from the physical damage. Even though I was sure that my story was the saddest ever when I first came to AA, I've heard some truly hair-curling tales since. But one thing is for sure: all of us were walking the same path with the same destination. It's funny, but I never tell anyone to "go to hell" anymore. As far as mourning the past, I don't. My sponsor gave me some great advice about dealing with the past: "It's okay to look back—just don't stare."

Unfortunately for many of us, AA is the water trough to our horse. It was always there for me, but I was too stubborn, mixed up, and scared to really give it a try. They say you can only come into AA when you're ready. That is mostly true, but not always. Some of us allow ourselves to be pressured into AA. That's not very likely to end well. Others keep moving the goalposts back and never seem to get to "ready." Others are so bereft of self-esteem, confidence, and hope that even walking into an AA meeting is too much for them. AA has a proven solution. But there was no reading, meditating, or wishing myself into sobriety. I had to actually walk in the door (see "The Meeting" on page 46).

CHAPTER 3

Why AA?

AA started working so fast and so well for me that I found myself unable to resist the temptation to dispense the odd bit of advice or expert opinion now and then. (This was typically something I read the night before.) I think this is harmless. I just get excited and want to share my newfound insight or tidbit with other AAs.

But publishing my thoughts on the finer points of a complex disease might be over the top. After all, I'm not a physician, a psychologist, a counselor, or even a particularly smart person. I am very opinionated and a recovering know-it-all. I am allergic to serious research, especially if glibness will get me by. But I do have one notable qualification: I've been an alcoholic for years. Alcoholism has been my day and night companion, and it nearly wrecked my life. Eventual death from alcoholism was a certainty for me if I hadn't gotten into AA. This is a disease that has had my full attention for a long time. Think of this as a tell-all book about a faithless lover: I lived with it. I felt the pain. I am entitled.

In the Beginning . . .

So let's start at the beginning: Two hundred million years ago, there was yeast. When a yeast cell came into contact with water and certain plant sugars from fruits, berries, or grains, it produced an enzyme. The sugars were converted into carbon dioxide and ethanol, which is the precursor of $400-a-bottle scotch. The busy little yeast cells continue to produce alcohol until they are eventually killed off by— you guessed it—acute alcohol poisoning. Alcohol has been claiming victims for a long time.

Early AAs strongly suspected that they suffered some kind of physical malady with regard to drink, even though medical wisdom at the time saw alcoholics as mental defectives and moral weaklings. Until their drinking caught up with them, AA's cofounders Bill Wilson and Bob Smith and many of the other first hundred AAs had been professionals who had managed their lives fairly well. But when it came to saying no to a shooter, they mostly could not. It was not until 1956 that the American Medical Association (AMA) formally acknowledged that alcoholism is a disease, and many years after that when medicine unlocked the body and brain chemistry of alcoholism. Bill and Bob (known by many AAs as Dr. Bob) didn't wait around for the medical community to embrace the disease theory of alcoholism. They included a chapter "The Doctor's Opinion"—in the original Big Book that identified alcoholism as a physical allergy. It was written by a lonely supporter of the idea, William D. Silkworth, MD. That breakthrough contributed immeasurably to the early success AA had with alcoholics who had previously been considered hopeless and doomed.

The disease concept of alcoholism is now fully accepted around the world and across medical disciplines (see the World Health Organization's definition of alcoholism on page 99). I did a fair amount of reading on the disease concept to reassure myself that I was not just a slacker, as I sometimes thought. But alcoholism is a recognized, progressive disease; it has a genetic element; and I have it. That knowledge allowed me to stop seeing myself as a bad person trying to be good and start seeing myself as a sick person trying to get well. Alcoholism is probably the only incurable, fatal affliction that most of us were happy to find out was actually a disease. If it were just a really bad personality flaw, AA would have been known as Losers Anonymous.

To AAs, alcoholism is a disease of body, mind, and spirit. Bill and Bob and the members of the original New York and Akron groups were probably the first alcoholics in America to come together in any numbers and openly discuss what was happening to them. One of their first conclusions was that alcohol was "cunning, baffling, powerful" (*Alcoholics Anonymous,* 58–59). But alcoholism "differs from virtually every other disease process in that it begins with symptoms indicating improvement" (*Beyond the Influence,* 54). These symptoms are intense pleasure, remarkably low levels of reaction to alcohol, ability to consume relatively large quantities of alcohol without feeling intoxicated, and marked absence of aftereffects. That was me for sure. I could hold my liquor. At least until I could no longer hold my liquor.

The fun began to ebb out of boozing fairly early in my drinking career. That was followed by a long period during which I drank regularly anyway and things started to go wrong in my life. Farther down the line, my body started re-acting badly. Hangovers got worse, sleep became more diffi-cult and uneven, my energy level plummeted, and I gained weight. I dealt with these symptoms by ignoring them. A little later on, I acquired a couple new friends: tinnitus and vertigo. I had a permanent ringing in my ears, and I was dizzy a lot of the time. Annual physicals were no fun. Laying off the sauce for a couple weeks before the exam didn't help much, and my bloodwork worried my doctor. By the end, I was drinking around the clock, I couldn't hold down food, and my blood pressure went through the roof. I was a mess.

Mentally, I was no better. In the beginning, drinking opened up a creative part of my brain that I couldn't seem to access otherwise. I really enjoyed writing or building stuff with a buzz on—I was calm and focused. But the law of di-minishing returns kicked in. I started noticing that my win-dow of creativity seemed to close if I had too much to drink. Also, while my actual handiwork did not suffer much at first, it did start to take a lot longer. Pretty soon, my creative win-dow opened and shut so fast I had to take notes if I expected to use any of my so-called insights. Eventually, the quality of my thinking cratered. I was often appalled to look at my scribblings or work the next day. My concentration was the last to go. At that point, there was little doubt that I was get-ting seriously dumb.

In addition, I was getting seriously paranoid, anxious, angry, resentful, grandiose, unrealistic, and generally de-tached from what was happening around me. I seemed to be spending more and more time fantasizing about settling scores or making millions. The same pointless thoughts (and really horrible old songs) played over and over in my head, and my memory went south.

As for my spiritual state, I had ignored this part of myself for many years. I believed in God because I was raised that way, and I thought of myself as a person who lived a moral life. But I was really only going through the motions. Alcoholism had put me in such a selfish place that there was no room for a spiritual life of any value.

That's how it was for me. Not every alcoholic drinks the same way. Some start young (I did); some start later in life. Some drink daily (I did); others are binge drinkers. The lucky ones eventually bottom out and face the fact that they're alcoholics. (In AA, we get to diagnose ourselves.) I've known heavy drinkers who deny that they're alcoholics and people who are not sure. I was both of those at one time or another. But for those of us who continue to drink despite the unambiguous warning signs and obviously harmful consequences, alcoholism is the eight-hundred-pound gorilla in most of our lives, and it can't be ignored or denied forever. The disease punched me in the nose until I finally bled.

Why Alcoholics Anonymous?

Alcoholism has been wrecking lives and killing people for thousands of years. It's strange to think that so little was known about it until fairly recently, especially when you consider how many people have been damaged over the millennia. To be fair, you could probably say the same thing about heart disease, diabetes, or cancer. But what's different about alcoholism is its most effective twenty-first century treatment modality is a lay fellowship founded by nonexperts early in the last century that does not rely on medications or medical procedures. While insulin, radiation, statins, antibiotics, chemotherapy, and other high-tech remedies have been marshaled against all the other major diseases, alcoholism is still most successfully treated in a nineteenth-century revival-tent support-group mode. Does anyone else think this is odd?

You'll hear over and over in AA that there's no use questioning how the program works. As if to settle the matter once and for all, AAs everywhere chant at the end of each meeting: "It works if you work it." When I was a newcomer, that sounded ridiculous to me. But as the days and months went by, I started to wonder whether trying to figure out AA was a waste of time. I was continually amazed at what AA gave me on a daily basis—clearly, my long-term life prospects were improving miraculously. AA was not unlike the watch I could not possibly build but that always told me exactly what time it was. Or, as a friend of mine calls AA, "the adjustable wrench that fits any nut."

But since I'm an alcoholic, I want to know things for myself. So I tried to unwrap, unwind, and understand the inner workings and hidden mechanisms of AA. Here's what I found.

I tried to imagine what it must have been like sitting around with the first AA groups in Akron or New York in the early 1930s. To a man (they were all men), they had been given up for dead by medicine. Each entered AA dry, but many couldn't stay that way and left. The ones who stayed seemed to know that sticking together somehow helped them stay sober. They sensed that there was a physical aspect to their alcoholism, and a few doctors were beginning to support that. But no one knew what the pathology was, much less how to treat it. Eventually, as they exchanged stories and experiences, they realized that they had partly thought their way into alcoholism. Maybe they could think their way out of it.

None of these insights qualified as a breakthrough on its own, but taken together, they were interesting. When these early AAs added spirituality to the mix, they started thinking in terms of treatment. If the alcohol craving was physical and an alcoholic could not reason it away, the only hope for these men was spiritual. At that time, there was a fair amount of popular psychology around promoting various mind-over-matter therapies, for example, New Thought, Positive Thinking, and Mary Baker Eddy's Christian Science. Each emphasized "letting go" or "surrender" to a higher power. At the same time, religious organizations like the Oxford Group were trying out spiritual remedies on drunks with some success. The spiritual principles behind these remedies probably influenced the design of the Twelve Steps. Finally, tent-show revivals across rural America were also flogging spiritual cures.

As the early AAs recognized that alcoholism had physical, mental, and spiritual components, the outline of a three-pronged treatment approach was coming into sight. The spiritual component catalyzed the other two, setting AA in motion and setting it apart from all other approaches. The early AA groups were different from what we think of today as support groups. The members were not only there to commiserate with each other but were also determined to find a remedy for their disease before they died of it. With that incentive, the early AAs identified three components of a possible treatment approach as they essentially talked their way through the problem.

First, they thought of alcoholism as a uniquely personal disease. All illnesses affect individual persons, but only alcoholism could actually be treated by the afflicted person—and *only* by that person. This kind of challenge appealed to the pioneer spirit in Bill and Bob. Second, they had to reconcile this individual challenge with their certainty that recovery could not occur in solitude. A group process was crucial. This required teamwork. Finally, Bill and Bob knew they had to pass on the AA message to ensure their own sobriety and the survival of the fellowship. A spirit of community led AA outside its tight-knit groups to alcoholics who still suffered. The publishing of the Big Book in 1939 took the message national and, eventually, global (see chapter 5, "The Twelve Steps and Twelve Traditions").

Think about this: A hundred regular Joes with a common fatal and incurable illness got together and decided that they were suffering in body, mind, and spirit. Their new concept of alcoholism was a medical breakthrough. They decided that they would treat themselves in a group setting on the basis of a dozen rules one of them thought up. The Twelve Step AA program is a treatment modality that is still in use, with proven success in 2 million cases of alcoholism. The early AAs applied three American civic virtues to do the job: pioneer spirit, team spirit, and community spirit. Pretty amazing.

But you may be thinking, *That's all very interesting, but what actually makes AA work?* Here's what I believe about that: AA fools us into thinking it's a self-help program long enough for our Higher Power to get hold of us and give us the real solution for alcoholism and the other demons that haunt our lives. Pretty amazing.

Some AA History

I'm a history buff, so I was interested in AA's historical literature. Imagine my surprise when I discovered that AA's history ended in 1955. Well, maybe its history didn't end, but the founding revolution did, and things got very quiet in AA after the mid-1950s. This is curious, because it was after 1955 that AA came to be known more and more around the world. I think history is both fundamental and irrelevant in AA. Here's why.

AA's early years are a fascinating tale of serendipity and remarkable spiritual intervention. It would make a good Hollywood movie, and actually did: *My Name Is Bill W.* starring James Garner and James Woods. AA's story from the mid-1930s to the mid-1950s was really the story of Bill Wilson and Bob Smith. Both were from Vermont and embodied old-time Yankee independence of mind and spirit. They were both accomplished in their chosen fields, finance for Bill and medicine for Bob. And they were both hardcore alcoholics.

In an organization that is famously anonymous, Bill and Bob managed to become famous. The Big Book—*Alcoholics Anonymous*—begins with the story of Bill's journey through alcoholism to sobriety. Bob's story leads off the testimonial section. Of the forty-three personal stories in the book, Bill's and Bob's are the only two in which the person is identified. The authoritative history of AA is Bill's biography, *Pass It On,* which was drawn from his own words. Bill wrote some 150 articles for the *AA Grapevine* magazine over the years, and a volume entitled *The Best of Bill* was published in 1988. He expanded on the AA program and set out a dozen organizing principles in his 1952 book *Twelve Steps and Twelve Traditions*. The point is that only two people have ever been well known both within the AA membership and publicly, and only one of them wrote its official history.

After Bob died in 1950, Bill recognized the risk of his own fame and concentrated authority. He made sure that AA was returned to its members as the largest, strongest, and most successful private fellowship in the world. That transfer happened over time, but the 1955 St. Louis convention is as good a date as any to mark the change. At the convention, Bill bestowed the three "legacies" on the membership: recovery (the Twelve Steps), unity (the Twelve Traditions), and service (the administrative structure that supports AA as an organization without governing it). In 1957, *Alcoholics Anonymous Comes of Age* was published, describing the three legacies in Bill's words. (If you're interested in AA history, there's a lot more than this.)

AA was David to alcoholism's Goliath. Bill and Bob were a unique and perfect duo, and their stories were parables of redemption. Bill was the visionary, and Bob was the conscience of AA. It's said that the two men never quarreled, although they occasionally disagreed about what to do next for the fellowship. They remained in character to the end. Bob's last words to Bill were "Let's not louse this thing up. Let's keep it simple." It's rumored that one of Bill's final laments about AA was that he wished the line "Rarely have we seen a person fail who has thoroughly followed our path" (*Alcoholics Anonymous*, 58) could be changed to "*Never* have we seen . . ." Bob Smith, ever practical; Bill Wilson, ever grand.

After Bill and Bob died, the shift from a high-profile narrative to relative institutional quiet is striking. I believe that Bill and Bob knew what they were doing, and that AA's low profile today has a purpose. The history of the early days still teaches the newcomer, but the most significant events in modern AA are the anniversaries of sobriety and other small individual victories in recovery. Bill and Bob turned AA's history over to us.

AA's Un-Structure

I was taught that you can unlock the mystery of any organization by understanding how it's structured, who leads it, and how its resources are generated and applied. In my work, I decoded many corporations, governments, and private trusts in just this way over the years. AA is the first enterprise I've ever encountered where this approach is absolutely useless.

It's not because AA operations are in any way shadowy. It keeps no records of any kind on its members, but there is no lack of institutional transparency. The fellowship is unique, not opaque. Since most AA outreach takes place on the local level, member oversight of corporate operations is the exception and not the rule. Very few of us are much concerned about the operations of headquarters as long as our group can be there for suffering alcoholics. Bill and Bob wanted the members to control AA, but they didn't want to foist a daily burden of management on us, and that's how it has turned out.

I'd be surprised if more than a handful of AAs know (1) who is the chair of the AA General Service Board of Trustees; (2) when the next AA area convention will be held and where; and (3) how the dollar they put in the basket at their last meeting was divided across AA operations. I'm committed to AA and my life may depend on its continued existence, but I can't answer any of those questions.

I did some research, and this is what I found out about AA's structure and organization. My sources were mostly other AAs (who provided a rainbow of contradictory information) and the AA General Service Office (GSO) in New York (which seemed pleased to be queried and responded with quiet professionalism and courtesy).

AA is structured like a wedding cake. Its democratic mandate emanates from the bottom layer, which is the group. Each group elects a general service representative, and they form district committees. District committee reps elect delegates to area assemblies (there are ninety-three AA areas in the United States and Canada). Finally, the area assemblies elect delegates to the annual General Service Conference (GSC). GSC delegates are elected to two-year terms; their service is staggered so that half the delegates are always new and half are experienced.

The GSC is the senior decision-making body of AA. Both the General Service Board of Trustees and the GSO answer to it. The AA GSO provides administrative support to AA groups around the world. The board of trustees supervises AA's two publishing operations: AA World Services and the *AA Grapevine.* The trustees also are responsible for handling the money received from the groups and from publishing.

That's what it looks like, but this is what I think is important: In the early days, AA was controlled by a board of trustees that had a voting majority of nonalcoholics. The hope was that AA would attract philanthropic contributions, and Bill and Bob knew that no one in their right mind would give money to an organization run by drunks. But philanthropy was not forthcoming in the early days. Instead, the steady commercial success of the Big Book and contributions from a growing membership through the 1940s and 1950s replaced efforts to solicit outside resources. Financial self-sufficiency was eventually formalized by the trustees and is the basis of AA's Seventh Tradition. AA's members now appoint the trustees, and alcoholics are the voting majority (fourteen to seven). The members truly own AA.

Decision making at the GSC is either by consensus (no dissent) or by "informed group conscience." The latter describes a unique AA way of making decisions from the individual group on up, in which all points of view are methodically considered, AA principles are applied, and "substantial unanimity" is achieved. If unanimity cannot be achieved, the issue is deferred. GSC decisions are most commonly in the form of "advisory actions" for the GSO or the board of trustees.

While ultimate authority in AA rests with the members, we carry that mantle lightly. In practice, the GSO operates as much on trust as through oversight. The same is true of the trustees. A corporation could not run this way for seven days, much less seven decades. The degree of devotion, competence, and trust that goes into the management of this 2-million-member organization is astonishing. After much study and thought, I've come to the conclusion that AA runs by magic. Magic is the only hypothesis left standing after all the others are eliminated. Or maybe it's this: if your life depends on the continuing existence of a certain fellowship that has saved you for today only, you will do whatever you can to see that the fellowship survives and prospers. For some of us, that will mean serving in AA's organizational structure for a time. For most of us, our service will be local. As with so much in AA, the choice is entirely ours.

Spirituality

I noticed in rehab that there seemed to be three general takes on spirituality in my group. Some people believed that being a career Lutheran or Hindu checked the spirit box, and they were comfortable with that. A second group, though honestly on the lookout for help, took a "not yet" or "not me" position. The third group assumed that spirituality was religion by another name and said no to both. Spirituality in AA is an important concept and not the easiest thing to understand. An open mind helped me finally get something going for myself.

If you are a religiously affiliated person, AA should not be too hard to accommodate in your existing belief system. If, on the other hand, you are agnostic, atheist, or just unimpressed with organized faith, AA's rebel spirituality might strike a chord. I was a little of both. You don't have to believe in an all-knowing supreme being for AA to work for you. It does help to recognize that you are not an all-knowing supreme being yourself. If you can get that far, you're ready to consider spirituality on its own merits.

Spirituality has come on the installment plan for me. I've moved toward acceptance of a few things today that would have seemed seriously out of bounds a year ago. At no point did I say to myself, *I have to digest this doctrine now or else I can't move forward.* It's not like that. Typically, as a certain part of the AA program began to work for me, I became willing to accept some of the spiritual baggage that was associated with that part. This step-by-step model was my choice and may not work for anyone else. For me, it's working a lot better than the death-by-the-pint lifestyle I brought to AA.

The journey to spirituality in AA is so personal that you can't use generalizations to describe it—with one apparent exception. A fair number of AAs I've compared notes with on this subject say they never seem to be actively aware of moving toward a more spiritual life. Unlike the rituals and rites of passage in organized religion, AA spirituality sneaks up on you. For example, one morning I might wake up feeling so damn good that I just want to be cheerful to everyone I meet. The next day I could find myself wildly grateful for the changes happening in my life. Before I know it, I truly want to be a better person and, miraculously, have the ambition to start in on the project. Recently, I've become interested in the higher-order functions of the mind and spirit. There it is! It seems that whenever I pursue any line of thinking on morality or living the right kind of life, I end up in the general vicinity of "the spirit." That's as mystical as I'm willing to get.

The following are two stories from the first days of my own recovery that illustrate what I mean about giving spirituality a try without expecting anything.

First story. In the late stages of my drinking career, I knew

I was in trouble. I had lost control and had no more fingers for the leaks in my levee. I was alone at home one morning, feeling toxically hungover and remorseful beyond belief. I was scared too. I decided that the time had come to call in reinforcements, so I set about praying. It was a typical foxhole message: "I'll do anything if you'll just get me out of this." When I had done all the pleading I could manage, I felt a strange calm. (Any calm was strange in those days, so I did notice it.) I also felt a certain gratitude. Maybe this would work. It did and it didn't. I sobered up enough to get fabulously drunk again and stayed that way for the better part of a month. I finally hit my bottom. I ended up in detox and then in rehab and then in AA.

Second story. For a couple months before I went into rehab, I was dropping in on AA meetings to keep the heat off at home. Since some of the meetings were during the day, I decided to tell a co-worker what was up so he could cover for my midday disappearances. My confidant sent me a nice get-well card the next day and promptly ratted me out to the boss. While I was in rehab, he went after my job. I was consumed with hatred for him. The chaplain at the rehab center suggested that I try praying for the guy to see if forgiveness could remove him from my tortured mind. I was skeptical, but after about a week of praying for him, my resentment just went away. I got focused on recovery and have never thought much about him since. This really happened, and no one was more surprised than I was at how it ended up.

I've come to believe that spirituality in AA is built on two foundations: acceptance and willingness. Here's how it crystallized for me.

It began with *acceptance.* Accepting that I'm an alcoholic is the price of my chair at an AA meeting for as long as I want to be there. It's also the essence of Step 1: "We admitted we were powerless over alcohol . . ." Acceptance of our alcoholism is the *only* part of AA that is considered a must. If we're not alcoholics, we don't belong in AA. If we're honestly not sure, we try some controlled drinking and see what happens. If we're pretty sure we're alcoholics but don't have sufficient desire to stop drinking, our drinking career is probably not over yet.

I thought accepting that I was an alcoholic would be a terrible personal defeat, a blow to my self-esteem that I wouldn't recover from. In another one of those peculiar AA twists, acceptance didn't mean defeat. It was a victory over my personal four horsemen of fear, dishonesty, selfishness, and resentment. I stopped judging my inner self by the standard of other people's outward appearance. I was so incredibly relieved when I finally "came out" that I had to control my urge to tell everyone around me.

Once I accepted myself as I was, it got a lot easier to accept the people and the world around me as they were. It was like driving out of a fog along the California coast. Everything is gloomy and disorienting, with no end in sight, and then, *bang,* all of a sudden it's clear and sunny. Accepting that I was an alcoholic was a little miracle for three reasons. First, I never thought I'd have the courage to do it. Second, it made me feel really good, not really bad. Third, after that, I found myself more willing to accept other things in life that also pleasantly surprised me.

Then there's *willingness,* which for me means taking risks.

I'm not talking about driving under the influence or playing games with other people's money or any of the other crazy things I did while I was drinking. The risks I now take require an open mind, and some of them take courage. There is no part of the AA program that requires more willingness than embracing spirituality. When I accepted that I could not beat booze alone, I didn't just give up. I was desperate enough to consider the possibility that a power greater than myself might be able to rescue me. That was a crushing realization for a person who was used to gutting it out. I feared pity more than failure.

Here's another AA story that says something important about willingness. The AA World Service chairman from 1951 to 1956, Bernard B. Smith, was on an airplane when the man seated next to him recognized him and began chatting about AA. In those days, the AA chair was always a nonalcoholic. The man asked Smith why it was that something as practical and admirable as the AA program couldn't have a wider application among people in general. Smith's famous one-word reply: "Motivation."

For me and for many other AAs, the path to motivation was a very rough road. Some of us lost everything before willingness to trust spiritual principles became an option. All of us lost something. As Smith also said, "The tragedy of our life is how deep must be our suffering before we learn the simple truths by which we can live." One of those simple truths is that we can break alcohol's hold at any time we wish.

The price is willingness. For a long time, I was stingy—I was only able to muster dribs and drabs of willingness. It was all I thought I could "afford" at the moment. The good news is that what I could afford was always just enough to keep my AA program going. Considering how clueless I was when I came into AA, it's lucky for me that even a little bit of willingness did the trick.

Catastrophe is not the only route to spirituality. Many folks get there in the context of a religion or personal philosophy. But it seems as though a lot of us in AA choose to rain hell down on ourselves to get to "Uh, this is not working out." A military friend suggested that my spiritual awakening in rehab sounded a bit like what happened to some of our pilots held by the North Vietnamese. The big difference, of course, is that I had the key to my cell all along. I believe Bernard Smith was right. It really is about motivation.

I like to know how things work, and maybe you do too. The way spirituality works in my life is through a simple reinforcing loop. Let's say I'm uncertain about changing jobs. This is just the kind of question I used to ponder over a fifth of vodka. Now I'm more likely to ask my Higher Power for a steer. In response, I may receive an inspiration on the subject that helps me decide. As I mull it all over, I might come to understand why one course of action is the right one. This happy cycle produces both gratitude for my connection with a Higher Power and an incentive to take another spiritual action in the future.

This loop of action-inspiration-understanding-action is admittedly a cautious approach to spirituality, but it's solid and it works for me. Some people get their spirituality all in one big bang. AA's cofounder Bill Wilson did, and in the beginning, he thought all AAs would too. Some people never get it, but maybe they're not really trying. As I said, I'm doing it on the installment plan. The longer I'm in AA, the more I believe that most of us baby-step into spirituality.

It's hard to describe how adding a spiritual dimension to my life makes me feel. Anything I say is bound to sound corny, naive, and maybe even made up. But 2 million other AAs are getting something spiritual out of the program too, and we can't all be wrong about this. So, here goes.

I can think of four tangible benefits of opening up to the spirituality that seems to be a natural result of working the Steps. First, the obsession and craving for alcohol left me. I never thought this would be possible. I believe it's a daily reprieve, but I have a little more confidence in it with every day that goes by. Second, I'm not so damn worried about everything. The fear and anxiety that were my constant companions as a drinker have largely been replaced by assurance and optimism. Not everything is settled in my personal affairs, nor is it ever likely to be. But I seem to know what to work on and how. I'm generally confident that things will turn out, and most things do. Third, I feel as though I've been let in on a few things that previously eluded me, such as these: What's really important? Who am I and what am I supposed to be doing? How do I make things better for me, mine, and others? Finally, I see the day-to-day world in a noticeably different way. My natural surroundings are more beautiful. People I meet are nicer and more interesting. Books I read seem to have more significance. I have new solutions for old problems, and not as many new problems. I'm happier, and I look forward to the routine and the surprises of daily life.

In AA, spirituality is its own reward. It is the source of energy to face my life with confidence. Rationalism, science, and all the other stuff in the reality family couldn't help me with my alcoholic despair because they exclude the personal and the private. Spirituality was the missing piece for me. I don't really know how spirituality works. For now, I've concluded that it's not knowable, only doable. Because I have to see and touch things to believe them, spirituality had to yield results for me in every important part of my life: family, job, friends, dreams, and aspirations. It has.

I don't worry about losing my shiny new spirituality. I assume I have it to use it. As long as my spiritual side gets regular exercise, I'll be okay. We alcoholics are happiest and most successful when we regularly do the right thing in three areas of our lives: for ourselves and our sobriety, for other alcoholics, and for everyone else. Simple, really.

CHAPTER 4

Some AA Basics

AA's philosophy and program will not dazzle you in the same way that the general theory of relativity might. But, as a combination of intellectual simplicity and spiritual depth, AA sets the gold standard. The program is laid out in the first 164 pages of the Big Book in simple declarative sentences, with helpful examples and an endearing earnestness. Intellectual gymnastics and academic showing off are nowhere to be found in the Big Book. Bill Wilson wrote the AA message on the basis of a solid liberal arts education, using a no-frills writing style and relying on the unvarnished group experience of the original AA members.

So where does the depth come from? I believe that the AA philosophy is profound, in part, because of what each person reads into it. We get some fairly clear and concise guidance on what to do. The Twelve Steps, for instance, are concisely worded and conveniently numbered. But each of us must decide how we feel about them and what they mean. This customizing option of the AA program is its true genius, in my view. Each person cobbles together a unique recovery. We try out different approaches with our sponsors and groups. In the end, if it works, it's the right answer. If not, we keep tinkering. This appealed to me, and I think it appeals to many other independent-minded AAs.

I believe that the following concepts are fundamental to the AA program. This is my own lineup, so I'm probably leaving out some people's favorites. However, I'm pretty sure that most AAs would agree that these concepts matter.

The Meeting

AA meetings did not work for me—at least not at first. I have since discovered through rigorous scientific trial that the success rate goes up dramatically if one does not attend AA meetings hammered. I learned something else about AA meetings along the way: there is absolutely no better way to start and sustain a recovery than by talking to another drunk about drunkenness. So simple. Who knew? Everyone's route to understanding the value of a meeting is somewhat different. Here's how I finally discovered the magic.

A week or so after I entered rehab, I was eligible for my first off-campus pass. I can't tell you how thrilled I was at the prospect of tooling down the road headed anywhere, as long as I was out. There were restrictions, of course. We had to go in groups of at least three (i.e., no boy-girl passes). We could go only to an AA meeting. Stops along the way were limited to the local Wal-Mart and the ice cream place. We had to be back within two hours. Sounds funny now, but at the time, it felt like a week in Paris. Eight of us piled into two cars and left the parking lot at the stroke of 7:00 p.m. The closest AA meeting was a yuppie get-together; they were used to giddy parolees from the nearby rehab dropping in. In fact, I learned later that a number of the regulars at that meeting were alums of our program. To my surprise, I felt welcome and more like a valuable trainee than the confused drunk I had been seeing in the mirror during the past months.

After the AA meeting, we raced over to Wal-Mart. For all our excitement, you would've thought it was Neiman Marcus. We scattered throughout the cavernous store, reveling in our temporary freedom and scooping up candy, alcohol-free mouthwash, magazines, and assorted junk. From there, we headed to the ice cream parlor and a chance to indulge our knack for overdoing it.

On the way "home," we passed a state trooper giving a field sobriety test to a hapless motorist. Old habits kicked in—we all held our breath and looked straight ahead as we approached the flashing lights and fearsome-looking cop. As we cleared the crime scene, our car erupted in the most juvenile shouting and honking that I've been a part of since my high school football team actually won a game. Not only were we not getting pulled over, it wouldn't have mattered!

We made curfew by a hair and found ourselves lingering by the nurses' station. No one wanted this evening of liberty to end. In an uncharacteristic burst of friendliness, I suggested that we all have a nightcap in the large common room. Hot coffee, a crackling fire, and not being smashed at 9:00 p.m. created a damn jolly mood, and the conversation turned to our previous lives on the outside.

As we exchanged tales of hopelessness and expressions of hope, the rush of candor created a bond among our little circle. Drake, a high school science teacher, started talking about the various places he hid his booze, and that seemed to bring out the rascal in all of us. Every hideout was more absurd than the last: in the toilet tank, with the grass clippings, in the vacuum cleaner bag, in a box of tampons. One guy kept his booze in a locked cabinet with the pesticides and rat poison (I don't recommend this at all). My personal favorite was the guy who could keep his liquor in plain sight in his basement because he had convinced his wife that there were mice down there. I mostly left my liquor in the liquor cabinet, but toward the end, I had to replace the bottles almost every day. This conversation was hilariously funny and cathartic at the same time.

The next day, I earnestly reported to my counselor how *therapeutic* it had been to open up to fellow inmates about my *problem*. She looked at me over her reading glasses and said, "Sounds like you went to your first real AA meeting." She was obviously referring to the nightcap session and not the actual AA meeting we had attended in town. I'd have to think about that.

It's generally accepted that the first AA meeting took place in May 1935, when Bill Wilson and Bob Smith got together by stunning coincidence in Akron, Ohio. Bill was in Akron leading a proxy fight for a machine tool company on behalf of investors back east. He had been sober for about six months, and a successful outcome in Akron might have put his investment career back on track. But the deal went south and Bill found himself wandering around the lobby of his hotel, trying to decide whether to go to the bar. Instead, he got on the phone and called a local clergyman named Walter Tunks. Bill said he was a "rum hound" from New York who wanted to talk to another drunk in order to stay sober himself.

After some false starts, he was directed to Henrietta Seiberling of the Goodyear Tire Seiberlings. Mrs. Seiberling had been praying for some kind of miracle for her drunken friend, Bob Smith. She thought Bill might be that angel and told him to meet Bob at her home, the Gate Lodge. When Bob sobered up the next day, the two men met.

The chemistry between Bill and Bob was powerful, and the idea for AA was hatched virtually on the spot. There's a lot more to this story, and versions of the meeting appear in almost every book about AA. I know some people who have visited the room in Akron where the two men met. They tell me that the place is uncommonly peaceful and has a good feeling to it.

That 1935 meeting had many of the characteristics of any AA meeting today. First, it was a get-together of people with "an honest desire to stop drinking" (*Alcoholics Anonymous,* page xiv). Alcohol was killing both Bill and Bob, so they clearly qualified for what is still the only membership requirement for AA. Crisis and craving often bring us to meetings—Bill was suffering from both that night in Akron. Also, going to a meeting is a choice. I go because I want to go, and I want to go because I know it will keep me sober. Bill made the same choice when he turned away from the hotel bar and walked to the telephone. Going to a meeting takes courage, and Bill showed his, especially when he phoned the socially prominent Seiberlings.

The fact that Bill and Bob met under such extraordinary circumstances was a colossal stroke of good fortune. The same phenomenon (if less dramatically) is at work at every AA meeting. The chance that I'll meet someone I should meet or hear something I should hear brings me back over and over. Most of us in AA believe that there is some nugget of wisdom or stroke of happy serendipity waiting for us at every meeting, if we just show up and pay attention.

I always leave AA meetings happier and with a bit more direction than when I walked in the door. Bob and Bill left their first AA meeting cheered and with a challenge they knew they had to undertake. For them, the challenge was to build a worldwide fellowship of alcoholics helping one another to get and stay sober. If they had known all the work that lay in store for them, they might've taken a pass. It is the good fortune of 2 million AAs that they accepted the challenge that lasted the rest of their lives. The bond they forged at that first meeting lasted a lifetime too.

How important is the AA meeting in the greater scheme of things? I believe it's the soul of AA. It's where the message is shared. It is a reservoir of experience, strength, and hope for newcomers and oldtimers alike. The meeting is the face of AA to thousands of people who are looking for something that they can't quite put their finger on. It's the core institution of the AA community for those of us who are already members. This loose collection of more than 100,000 quasi-independent groups, meeting in locations around the globe, is the solid foundation of the largest single fellowship in the world. AAs on oil rigs can participate in meetings via e-mail, and our magazine, the *AA Grapevine,* is referred to as a "meeting in print." The group ensures AA unity through its independence. We recover by helping others to recover. Much of this occurs at meetings.

There are various kinds of meetings. The best known is the discussion meeting; it can be open (anyone can attend) or closed (limited to people who have a desire not to drink, that is, alcoholics). There are discussion meetings specifically for men, for women, for gay men, and for lesbians. There's also the speaker meeting, at which a member of AA tells his or her story (see "drunkalog" on page 108). And the Step meeting, where members talk specifically about the Steps and Traditions. And the Big Book meeting, where AA's basic text is discussed.

Any AA is welcome to attend any meeting, with the exception of gender- or sexual-orientation-specific meetings. Many people pick a "home group"—that's the meeting you go to regularly, where you know people well, and where you typically celebrate your sobriety anniversary. You can find out about local meetings on the Internet or by calling Alcoholics Anonymous. There's a listing in almost every town in the United States and in many cities around the world. As someone who thought for a long time that AA meetings were for losers, I come humbly to the task of setting the record straight. Please trust me: the people you will meet at an AA meeting are not losers. We are the fortunate ones, and we are damn grateful and happy about it. The unfortunate ones are still out there suffering, if they're alive at all. I admit that meetings can seem a little odd at first. But I was pretty odd myself when I walked through the door.

Before I went to rehab, I was asked to leave an AA meeting for being obnoxiously drunk. (Inebriated people do sometimes come to meetings. They don't fool anyone, and if they sit quietly, they're usually not booted out.) This episode was so mortifying that I credit it with triggering the month-long bender that finally put me in detox and then rehab.

Since rehab, a lot of really good things have happened to me at AA meetings. I met my sponsor at a meeting and seemed to know on the spot that this was the person who had what I wanted and would show me how to get it. I can't count the number of "aha moments" I've had in meetings. I can honestly say that while I've come into some meetings pretty grouchy, I've never left in anything but good cheer. That was not true of all my experiences with bars and parties.

A lot of people who decide to give AA a whirl follow the suggestion of going to ninety meetings in the first ninety days. This may sound like overload, but an hour a day is probably much less time than you used to spend drinking. I've read that some MDs think it takes heavy drinkers about ninety days without a drink to collect their marbles.

The magic of any AA meeting anywhere is the same spark that ignited AA when Bill Wilson and Bob Smith met in Akron or that fired me up in rehab, when I first got honest with others about alcohol. It's one drunk talking to another drunk about how to get undrunk. That's what it is.

One more thing. I was really lucky to hit just the right AA meeting for me early in my recovery. Meetings, like the people in them, have personalities of their own. It's fairly important to feel comfortable in the meetings you attend early on, although time and location are important factors too. My free advice on this is to shop around until you find a meeting or two that seem right for you. This is not, of course, license to find all meetings wanting and repair to the local saloon while AA gets its act together. Being human, I like some meetings better than others. But I've never been to a meeting that was not welcoming and attended by people who care about each others' sobriety.

The Sponsor

One of the essential components of a successful AA program is having a solid sponsor. So how come sponsors are not mentioned in the Twelve Steps? Bill and Bob knew that someone had to bring the AA message to each person, so the concept of the sponsor was present in the early annals of AA, although it wasn't called sponsorship. Remember, AA is a little like a treasure hunt, and we have to figure out some things for ourselves.

Bill always referred to Ebby Thacher, who came to him with the Oxford Group message of redemption in 1934, as his sponsor. Bob called Bill his sponsor. Men who entered the Akron Group in the 1930s and 1940s typically came in with the endorsement of an existing member to protect everyone's anonymity. Chapter 7 in the Big Book ("Working with Others") is an early version of what it means and what it takes to bring the AA program to a drunk. That is the core task of sponsorship.

From the beginning of my association with AA, people told me how important it is to get a sponsor. No one told me much about what to look for in a sponsor or how to approach one, so I got a little tense about the process. I tried to figure out who the best all-around member was in the group I was in and sign that person up. My sponsor later told me that he agreed to sponsor me out of curiosity, wanting to find out whether I was really as big an ass as I seemed in early sobriety. I was damn lucky.

Here are a few characteristics I value in my sponsor and would recommend to others. It's my list only, but it might help you narrow the field. Don't worry about being rejected. Most AAs are at least a little bit flattered to be asked, and all of us know that sponsoring someone else is the best way to stay sober ourselves.

- *Model.* Look for someone who seems to be living the AA program, as far as you can tell. Don't go on a saint-hunt, but keep an eye out for members who participate, show kindness to others, seem comfortable in their own skins, and so on. Seek out someone who's walking the walk.
- *Mentor.* You'll be taking a fair amount of direction and some advice from your sponsor, so look for someone with whom you'll be comfortable (at least temporarily) in a subordinate or student role. This was not easy for me, and I don't think I'm alone. AAs often have difficulty listening and learning from others. They say in AA that it's harder to recover with your mouth open, and I'm living proof of that.
- *Sherpa.* This sounds corny, but recovery is a mountain for some of us and going up with someone who has already made the climb is not a bad idea, much like the Tibetan Sherpas who guide climbers up Mt. Everest. A good sponsor will not only show you the route but also alert you to bumps in the road, detours, and steep spots. Having an encouraging guide that you trust is a good way to journey through AA.
- *Teacher.* A good sponsor will usually be a good teacher too. That means understanding the program and being able to pass it on. Sometimes you'll be impressed by

how a veteran member speaks about the program at a meeting. That person might be a good sponsor for you. But don't get anxious. When the student is ready, the teacher will appear.

- *Confidant.* You're going to share some fairly wretched stuff about yourself with your sponsor, so do what you can to assess the person's discretion before you start. If at any time along the road to recovery your sponsor breaches confidentiality, show him or her the door.

- *Friend.* In the beginning, there was a certain distance between me and my sponsor because we were in a teacher/student relationship. As my recovery progressed, we became friends. If that happens for you, great. If not, it's no big deal.

There are a couple intangibles that enter into the sponsor selection that I'll mention for what they're worth. First, look at a prospective sponsor and ask yourself whether he or she has something important that's missing in your life. For me, it was calm. If you don't see something like that, keep looking. Second, things seem to go better if the chemistry is good. My sponsor and I hit it off and, as time wore on, realized that we had much in common. For example, I needed someone with a sense of humor. In fact, I can't imagine doing the AA program with someone who doesn't think that life can be pretty funny.

There are a few things that a sponsor is *not* that most of us probably know intuitively but may bear mentioning.

A sponsor is not a nanny. If you want to drink, drug, or otherwise wreck your life, you probably will, and it's not your sponsor's job to babysit you if you're still using. AA will be waiting for you when you're finished, if you want to try again.

Sponsors are not bankers. Because we're irresponsible when we're drinking, many AAs find themselves "a little short" coming into the program. In my experience, most of us overcome that. In fact, I'm willing to bet that AAs are better credit risks than the general population. But covering you until payday is not in your sponsor's job jar.

Don't expect your sponsor to referee conflicts between you and your spouse, boss, friends, and so on. Your sponsor works with *you*. You work with everyone else in your life.

Finally, your sponsor is more likely to drive you nuts by withholding advice than by giving it. In early sobriety, sponsors can look like the most together people. They are not. They just work harder and smarter at the same kinds of things that bother you. When I ask my sponsor for advice, I usually get, "Well, I don't know what you should do, but this is what I did in a similar situation."

How do you actually get a sponsor? This is tricky, so pay attention: you ask. Yes, just ask. Sometimes at AA meetings, the chair will call for a show of hands of those willing to sponsor. Remember, boys for boys and girls for girls (unless you're a gay man or a lesbian, then it's the opposite). This is not Match.com. If you're not sure that you're making the right choice, either wait a few days or ask the person to be your temporary sponsor. This is a common way to try out a partnership.

What if you ask someone and they don't accept, for whatever reason? For example, many sponsors limit themselves to a certain number of sponsees. Don't be deterred. Just keep asking. What if a sponsor relationship doesn't work out? This is hard because of human nature and feelings, but your highest priority is your recovery. If your recovery is not being well-served in the relationship, end it. If your sponsor is a solid AA, that won't be a problem. Final point: When will you be ready to sponsor others? You have to be asked first, and at that point, I believe that we just know we're ready.

For me, recovery from alcoholism has a lot to do with coming out of isolation and reconnecting with the world. I think that's true for many of us. My sponsor has done more than any other person to walk me back into the human race. Freedom for us alcoholics comes in the company of others. There is no recovery alone.

Ironies and Paradoxes

There are a lot of *ironies* in AA—things that are the opposite of what I would have expected. It's a program to quit drinking, but you're never told to quit. It's focused on a medically defined illness, but you're encouraged to diagnose yourself. A connection with God or a Higher Power is the key to success, but you can define your Higher Power any way you want. It's an organization, but there are no real rules or leaders. It's a nonprofit that does not accept philanthropy. Being an AA is only for certain people, but anyone can join. There are 2 million members all over the world, but the fellowship is not advertised or promoted. As I did the Steps, I got used to the ironies that seemed to pop up. In fact, I came to appreciate them—they made things more interesting.

Then there are the *paradoxes*. A paradox is a self-contradictory proposition that may, in fact, be true. You'll hear them repeated singly or together over and over in your AA travels. I think AAs like paradoxes because they reflect our own struggle to reconcile contradictory and opposing currents in our lives and create some kind of harmony. A lot of what I thought was true while I was drinking turned out not to be. Ultimately, these four simple statements held profound truth for me.

- *Surrender to win.* For me, this meant giving up self-will and letting my Higher Power take the lead. Self-will and self-centeredness were the taproots of my destructive lifestyle. I was convinced that I could run everything, and this led to one disaster after another. By the time I got around to looking for help, my life was in real trouble. I had to surrender to the program, to the group meetings, and to God to turn things around.

  Surrender in this sense implies enlightenment, not defeat. I could only surrender through courage, because fear would never permit surrender. Once I turned my life and will over to the care of God, important things started to work again for me. This cause-and-effect relationship between surrender and victory over life's demons and challenges is what keeps me working the AA program.

- *Suffer to get well.* It's a sad truth of alcoholism that most of us have to suffer a great deal before we can take the road to recovery that was there all along. Hopeful talk about finding the DNA marker for alcoholism gives me no hope. I knew from my family history that alcoholism might be lurking out there waiting to claim me next. It didn't matter. I had to prove to myself and to many people around me that I was afflicted before I could accept the AA message. Hitting my personal bottom was the starting gun for my recovery, and the memory of what it was like to be a drunk is what keeps me going. I had to feel real pain.

- *Give it away to keep it.* AA is not a solitary program. Participation in meetings was my single greatest source of inspiration and enthusiasm for my recovery, and the relationship with my sponsor was crucial to working the Steps for the first time. And once I started to "get it," I began to see that my grip on sobriety and serenity depended entirely on reaching out to other alcoholics who suffered. This chain of one alcoholic helping the next ensures the continued existence of the fellowship and the groups that, in turn, ensure my own sobriety. My life depends on it.

- *Die to live.* This sounded over the top until I gave it some thought. The "me" who had to die off was the self-centered, arrogant, fearful, deceitful, sickly drunk. I traded that life for an infinitely better existence built on physical, mental, and spiritual health. Seeking God's will for me and caring about others have opened fabulous possibilities in all areas of life. And I really mean life: love, friends, success, health, serenity, strength, willpower, creativity, purpose, fun, beauty, and a hundred other things that were out there all the time. I just couldn't see them because I was drunk.

The Promises

As an alcoholic, I knew a thing or two about promises. I'd made plenty of them and had actually intended to keep most. I just couldn't do it, and that made me feel terrible. A couple of drinks usually helped.

Then there were the AA promises they were flogging in rehab. As a skeptic and experienced promise-breaker, I was not buying them. This was the bait in the bait-and-switch. I conveyed my doubts to my counselor during group, careful not to upset my fellow inmates who were still looking for the quarter under their pillow. My counselor gave me her usual kind smile, "More will be revealed, A.J. Be patient." Deferred gratification was never my strong suit.

The teaching text of the Big Book is 164 pages long. The rest of the book is mostly stories. With sales of almost 28 million, Bill's words have been pretty well sliced and diced during the past seventy years. It's remarkable how well it has stood up. Someone went through the text and counted the number of promises made to us eager readers: 132. Whether that's exactly right or not, there are a lot of promises in the Big Book. That shouldn't surprise us—Bill Wilson was nothing if not a great salesman.

I went through three stages of reaction to all these promises. First, I was very resentful that such obvious flimflam could be perpetrated on us vulnerable drunks. (I was easily upset in those early days.) Then I started wanting the promises to be real. This is what I call my "what-if stage" of recovery. I'm in the third stage now: I have total confidence that the promises will come true if I'm diligent and honest in working

the program. How do I know? Many have already material-
ized for me. Remember, as a drunk, I'm smarter than you are.
Unless you're a drunk too, and then we can argue about it. I
always demand proof.

The greatest hits of the promises lineup, in my opinion,
are the ones on pages 83–84 of the Big Book. You know these
promises are Best in Show because they're known simply as
"The Promises":

> We are going to know a new freedom and a new hap-
> piness. We will not regret the past nor wish to shut the
> door on it. We will comprehend the word serenity and
> we will know peace. No matter how far down the scale
> we have gone, we will see how our experience can ben-
> efit others. That feeling of uselessness and self-pity will
> disappear. We will lose interest in selfish things and gain
> interest in our fellows. Self-seeking will slip away. Our
> whole attitude and outlook upon life will change. Fear of
> people and of economic insecurity will leave us. We will
> intuitively know how to handle situations which used to
> baffle us. We will suddenly realize that God is doing for
> us what we could not do for ourselves.

There's little I can say about the promises that they don't say
for themselves. I demanded proof that they could be fulfilled,
and you should too. You might try skipping the resentful/
skeptical stage and jump right to the what-if stage. But if you're
a true alcoholic, you probably won't be able to do that, and
that's okay.

Dog-ear page 83 and check it out every once in a while.

As the Big Book says, "we will be amazed before we are half way through."

Progress, Not Perfection

I've never heard anyone say, "I plan to stay in AA forever." Just as our reprieve from the alcohol craving is a daily event, our membership in AA renews every twenty-four hours. It's not unusual for people to stop coming to meetings for a while or for good. Sometimes they fall victim to complacency and old thinking; sometimes after years of sobriety, they feel sure that they're cured and it's okay to rejoin the party. The best way to avoid "going out" is to know where AA is taking us and to enjoy the journey. "Progress, not perfection" is AA's Global Positioning System. This is how it works.

Of the Twelve Steps, only one—the first one—needs to be taken perfectly and fully: *We admitted we were powerless over alcohol—that our lives had become unmanageable.* The other eleven Steps set out ideals toward which we work. No AA is expected to fully execute those eleven Steps. Honest effort and solid progress are enough to secure our sobriety and good standing with our Higher Power and our fellows. As long as we're making progress, we're making the grade in AA.

Of course, there are as many definitions of "progress" as there are AAs. This seeming chaos is built into the program. AA's trademark do-it-your-own-way approach is what keeps me and a lot of other members in the fold. If performance benchmarks were imposed on us as a group, plenty of us would mutiny on the spot. I worked diligently on the Steps for two main reasons, and neither had anything to do with the expectations of other AAs. First, I had become convinced that I could not beat alcohol doing what I was doing and that my personal status quo was not sustainable. Second, my AA program started to produce positive results very fast. I could see that my life was getting better. There's no substitute for tangible results. This cause-and-effect relationship between action and results is a powerful incentive for many of us in AA. We enjoy our journey.

Okay, let's say that it feels good to work the program. Where does the program take me? Like most alcoholics, I wanted whatever it was now, not later. The Big Book is full of cautions about our lack of patience and immature impulsiveness. Bill recognized this in himself and knew there had to be a way to engage the recovering alcoholic over the long term. He also understood that if you don't know where you're going, any road will get you there. He had walked a few detours himself. Amazingly, he figured out how the AA journey should go.

Short-term, tangible results and a known spiritual destination give the AA program depth and meaning. I don't have to reach total enlightenment to enjoy the benefits of my program today, but it is the steady progress toward AA's ideals that engages my intellect and ambitions for the long haul. Considering how much planning I put into things like career, family, finances, and parties, I never had any conception of what kind of person I wanted to be tomorrow or next year. I thought that if I paid attention to my material life, my spiritual life would fall into place. Actually, it's the other way around.

I've found that this is not a bad way to run my affairs. It's entirely in keeping with AA's "one day at a time" philosophy, and it reconciles my need for a life road map with my alcoholic requirement for reward. Feeling good every day is great, but it's not enough. I have to be going somewhere that's worth getting to. Progress, not perfection.

CHAPTER 5

The Twelve Steps
and Twelve Traditions

Despite a name that sounds like a 1950s British mystery novel, the Twelve Steps and Twelve Traditions are the mother lode of recovery from booze. If 2 million people were rescued from any other fatal illness, by any remedy at all, you wouldn't be able to keep it on the shelves. Although I didn't see things with this kind of clarity as my drinking spun out of control, my choices were clear: have another drink and think about AA, or give it a whirl. I chose to have another drink and give it a whirl.

The Twelve Steps

There are two things about the Twelve Steps that every newcomer must understand before undertaking the miracle of recovery. I didn't know either of them until recently, so maybe you don't really have to know them early on, but it might help.

First, the Steps are a suggested program, not a program of suggestions. The distinction is important. For example, I like to assemble things I get from Target by looking at the picture of the finished product on the box. To me, any leftover parts are just spares. The message here is do not cherry-pick the Steps for the easy ones or skip the ones that make you tense up. Do them in order, do them honestly, and do them all.

Second, suggested program means just that—it is a suggestion. If AA is a quilt, the way each of us ultimately works the program is our square. Drunks are not born followers, so there are as many roads to recovery as there are AAs. You can do the Steps quickly or slowly, and many people do them over again every so often. I recommend getting the first three under your belt without delay, but you make the call. As long as real sobriety is where you want to go and you resist shortcuts, the Steps will get you there.

I started the Steps in rehab. My counselor set getting through Steps 1, 2, and 3 in four weeks as "recovery milestones" in my treatment plan. I viewed my treatment plan as my get-out-of-jail card, so I took every word in it literally. I wasn't willing to risk my release papers twenty-eight days down the road, so I threw myself into the work. My motivation was impure, I admit.

Whatever your incentive is, I recommend putting your shoulder into the Steps.*

Step 1

"Okay," I said, pulling out my Big Book, "let's get going on these Steps." I was doing fine until I actually started. Step 1 flummoxed me big time. First of all, I expected that the first Step would be something like "Thou shalt not drink the evil grape

---

* The Twelve Steps on pages 67–86 are reprinted from *Alcoholics Anonymous*, 4th ed. (New York: AA World Services, Inc., 2001), 59–60.

ever again." Not only was quitting drinking not in the first Step, it is nowhere to be found in any of the following eleven. My keen intellect—sharpened by heavy doses of Librium in early treatment—told me that a trick was being played here. I read Step 1 carefully:

> We admitted we were powerless over alcohol—that our lives had become unmanageable.

Out of thirteen words, I was having trouble with four of them. First of all, why did I have to "admit" anything? Why couldn't I simply think or suspect? And "powerless"— wasn't that a little strong? After all, I was in rehab. Wasn't that a powerful thing to be doing? Also, saying I had a problem with "alcohol" in general irked me. I had drunk all kinds of booze, including beer, wine, tequila, and Southern Comfort, without more than the occasional regret or hangover. My problem was with vodka. Finally, I really resented being asked to say my life had become "unmanageable." I had never missed a mortgage payment. Some of the guys at rehab joked that in their version of Step 1, it was ". . . that our wives had become unmanageable." I thought that was funny and more realistic than saying my entire life had gone off the rails.

I brought my misgivings about Step 1 to group therapy, certain that major editorial changes in the text would result from my thoughtful critique. Bill Wilson had obviously fallen prey to purple prose when something calmer would appeal more to sensitive people like us. I explained my suggested improvements of the text carefully to my group. I could almost handle the counselor's smirk, but the guffaws of my fellow drunks were heartbreaking. "You are so in denial! You really don't get it, do you, A.J.?"

The group's rejection of my absurd self-justification was a blinding flash of the obvious for me. I *was* in denial. Big chunks of my life were starting to crumble: family, work, health, self-respect. I was scared. Innumerable attempts to drink like other people had failed, and I was beaten. I was in rehab and I was doing the Steps because I *had* to in order to survive. I was not going to die tomorrow, but I was doomed unless I jerked myself into another reality. I was an alcoholic and I belonged in AA.

Step 2

Came to believe that a Power greater than ourselves could restore us to sanity.

I went to Sunday school and church growing up, and it was a positive experience, so I didn't react the way some other patients in rehab did to the Higher Power thing. I got the feeling that some of my fellow sufferers had been let down by the Big Guy over time, and some carried quite a grudge. Throughout my drinking career, I'd prayed for everything from a burst of sobriety at the DUI stop to strong onions on my hoagie. It was the idea that I was somehow insane that alerted my psychic defenses. I knew that schizophrenia and bipolar disorder were forms of insanity, and I knew I didn't have either of those. So how come AA was calling me crazy?

After getting my wagon fixed by my group on Step 1, I was a little less strident when I inquired about the term "sanity," and the explanation made sense. Insanity, I was told, is doing the same thing over and over and expecting a different result. In my case, this meant drinking day after day with the expectation that I could control it, but always ending up blotto. Add to this the fact that drinking this way would eventually kill me, and it does suggest a kind of nuttiness.

God again. If you can get by "insanity" but have trouble swallowing the Higher Power concept, do not despair. Lots of newcomers feel this way, and there is even a chapter in the Big Book aimed at agnostics. After all, if your average drunk was much of a believer to begin with, there might not be so many of us. One gimmick to get past God-skepticism is to use the AA group itself as a sort of Higher Power for starters. My feelings changed a lot as I went through the Steps, and so might yours. Just accepting that I was suffering from an affliction that I couldn't address alone was enough at first. Later on I got more serious about enlisting long-term help. The point is just that we have a problem we can't fix by ourselves and there is something out there that is bigger than we are that can help us. No one has to get anointed in AA.

Step 3
Step 3 is the hardest Step for many people. It's also the Step with the biggest payoff, in my view.

> *Made a decision to turn our will and our lives over to the care of God* as we understood Him.

Not all alcoholics are jackass-stubborn, self-centered, and arrogant, but scientific research has revealed that about 90 percent are. That makes Step 3 the matador's cape of the program.

That was my situation. After admitting that I was "powerless," I was not ready to turn anything as valuable as my life and will over to anyone. I was trying to rebuild my life and stiffen my will, not send them to the cosmic recycle bin. But I learned that in Step 3 (as in a lot of AA) a little bit of willingness goes a long way. All it really took for me was an honest look at how I was doing running my own life on the strength of my own will. It was not a pretty picture, as they say. Also, there was plenty of wiggle room in the wording of Step 3 to allow me to get my toe in the water. I was only committing to make a "decision" to do something, not necessarily to actually *do* it. I was only committing my life and will to the "care" of a Higher Power, not actually including the deed and title. Finally, I was dealing with God as I understood him, and that was a comforting loophole.

I was a coward with all the scruples of a personal injury lawyer, but I managed to turn the wheel over to someone who could actually drive. As time went on, I became more comfortable with the idea that I don't know it all and that—as with everything in AA—the results tell us all we need to know.

Step 4

Steps 1, 2, and 3 got my head in the game and prepared me for the action part of the program: Steps 4 through 9. Step 4 is my personal favorite, because this is where Bill and Bob showed what a great sense of humor they had and what a short walk it is to reality for most of us, even after years of drinking. For some reason, many people are scared to death of Step 4. I walked around it a few times before getting started, but I'm here to tell you that it's not that bad. And there's a surprise ending that's worth the agro.

Made a searching and fearless moral inventory of ourselves.

Many people's reaction to this Step is "I'd rather not." For a short sentence, it's packed with strong words. But Step 4 appealed to me precisely because of the powerful language. I saw myself as the fearless type, and I was pretty sure that a moral inventory would confirm my largely positive self-concept. This is a good example of what they call "alcoholic thinking." I know a fair number of AAs who stalled on Step 4 out of pure avoidance. The joke is that it takes "two years and a Sunday afternoon" to complete Step 4. My advice is not to waste the two years.

Once you're ready, you'll need a #2 pencil and some sheets of lined paper to optimize your success. Start by making a list of all the people who piss you off and why. This is really therapeutic and will appeal to most alcoholics. I scribbled and sharpened and scribbled and sharpened until my desk was an inch deep in spleen. What a list of rogues and rascals! Hard to believe I'd been friendly at one time or another with most of them.

At this point, my sponsor told me to add another column where I list what it was that each person in each circumstance threatened among my closely held valuables: security, self-esteem, sexual relations, personal relationships, and so on. The people on my list were bastards, all right. So far, so good.

Next my sponsor told me to add a column listing my part in the various problems. This is where I started to get a little nervous. I thought this was about people who pissed me off. But I wanted to see what would happen next, so I soldiered on and did as I was told. Sure enough, I had set the stage for a lot of these troubles and was flat-out responsible for the rest. There was only one explanation for that: damn booze. Fortunately, I was no longer a drinker.

Well, it turns out that it wasn't the damn booze. The last column my sponsor had me add was one where I listed my particular "character defects" that were responsible for each problem or trashed relationship. Self-centeredness, pride, envy, lust, procrastination, and fear were big for me. The actions of the other person were only part of the problem in most instances and irrelevant in the rest. My internal GPS had been so cockeyed that I rarely understood my actual position in the real world of people, places, and things. My way of thinking about what mattered in life began and ended with me. When other people were not following my script and choreography, I got angry at their lack of team spirit and good sense. No wonder I was frustrated and anxious all the time, always in need of a drink or ten and another dose of self-delusion.

Step 4 led me to admit a huge possibility: maybe other people did not think the way I did. I always knew that opinions on this or that varied among human beings, but I never questioned that my own take on what was important in life—especially my life—was essentially shared by the rest of the planet. So my original list of people to punch in the nose ended up being a list of folks who probably deserved a fruit basket and a hug. If that isn't funny, I don't know what is.

It was interesting to find out so much about myself, but I

noticed that most of the news was pretty bad. I needed to start fixing some of this stuff. As it turned out, help was on the way.

Step 5

Admitted to God, to ourselves, and to another human being the exact nature of our wrongs.

Step 5 sounds a lot like confession and probably does come from the ancient religious tradition of making a clean breast of it. As intimidating as coming clean sounds to most of us, especially alcoholics, I was ready to get on with it after all the enforced honesty of Step 4.

Two things about Step 5 were important to me, and I'll pass them along for what they're worth. First, be thorough about it and resist the totally human temptation to leave the most awful or embarrassing things out. But if you do fudge a few things, don't panic. I know many AAs who've gone back for a second session when they were ready to unload the more difficult things. Also, you can do part of your list with someone like your sponsor and the rest with someone else, like a member of the clergy or a doctor, who is used to hearing the kinds of things you have to say . . . and worse. My favorite trick for overcoming the embarrassment of a nasty set of confessions is the AA who went to a meeting in another town, asked a total stranger to listen to her Fifth Step, and never went back to that meeting. But however you handle it, do handle it. If you leave things pending for too long— especially the things that haunt you the most—it will be that much harder to get your life straightened out.

The second part of completing Step 5 that was important to me was picking the person I'd go through it with. My choice was pretty easy, since my sponsor and I had hit it off and built a reservoir of mutual trust. Your Step 5 partner must be discreet. If you have any doubts, keep looking. This is one of those "don't try this at home" things. Step 5 is serious and not without risks. Be sure before you start that your confidant is solid.

The actual telling of my story to another human being was nothing like the humiliation I had imagined. My sponsor nodded and laughed me through it, and by the time I was finished, I was pretty sure of two things: I was not a bad person and I was not alone.

What a relief.

Step 6

If you let it, Step 6 can open the way to the life we all seem to be seeking in one way or another. It worked that way for me. While I was drinking, I always wanted to be self-assured, fearless, serene in the midst of chaos, confident about the future, loved, and respected. A few drinks usually set me at peace about all that, but doubts and fears would return each morning. As my drinking increased, my worries got bigger and felt more real, while my ability to overcome what scared me diminished. The answer was always to go to the gauzy world of alcohol.

As I looked at Step 6, I thought I saw a way out.

Were entirely ready to have God remove all these defects of character.

Remember, how I defined God was entirely up to me, as long as I accepted that there was a power greater than myself that could help me get to where I wanted to go. To get started, my sponsor suggested that I go to a quiet place and review my work so far, with special attention to thoroughness and honesty. This was a good idea, and I recommend it. The first five Steps are a wild ride for most of us, and a psychic time-out was just what I needed at this point. I was pretty satisfied with my effort so far, and the prospect of shedding a few weaknesses and picking up a strength or two was good motivation.

I was probably jumping the gun a little—the process of removing defects is a lifetime journey. The AA doctrine is that Step 1 (admitting we're powerless over alcohol) is the only Step we must accomplish 100 percent and right now. The other eleven are ideals toward which we strive. My old impatience kicked in at the idea of wasting time being "ready," but my sponsor came to the rescue. He suggested that I simply add a three-letter word to the end of Step 6: "now."

Asking God to make me a better person was such a personal departure that even preparing to start down that road was a high-order spiritual experience. My prior spiritual life had been all about seeking divine intervention on my own behalf. Mainly, I wanted help getting stuff. By the time I'd finished lining my head up with Step 6, I was not only ready to see the end of some of my character defects, but I also had come to believe that this was actually going to happen.

Step 7

I have a friend who's a nun. When I first met her, I asked what order she was in. Without missing a beat, she answered, "Sisters of Humility and damn proud of it!" While I was drinking, humility had absolutely no role in my life. As far as I was concerned, it was the refuge of underachievers and cowards. Funny . . . when I drank, I became both.

Humbly asked Him to remove our shortcomings.

Step 7 seemed to throw a monkey wrench into my plans for a quick return on Step 6. Humility was clearly the price of admission. My first reaction was determination to become more humble than anyone else in AA so I could have my defects removed without delay. I was clearly missing the point.

My problem with humility is shared by many AAs—it sounds too much like humiliation. But with the power to jettison my defects so near, I knew I had to try to work out a distinction. I settled on this: Humiliation is something I feel when other people think I'm an ass. Humility is something I feel when I know that I'm capable of being or not being an ass. I was very proud of my definition of humility, so I knew I still had some work to do in this area (see "humility versus humiliation" on page 119).

I was ready to start asking for some relief from my personal case of spiritual leprosy. This is where I learned how to ask nicely. Having grown up in organized religion, I thought I had mastered prayer at an early age. My technique was the "letter to Santa" method. I invariably prayed for something concrete: a promotion, fame, acceptance, a flatter tummy. In return, I promised either to do or not do something. I also sent up the occasional foxhole prayer asking for an emergency bailout. It was usually a plea not to get caught doing something, in return for a postdated promise to be good.

Step 7 brought me to a very different place. Here I was

asking for the removal of character defects so that I might become a better person. Of course, I believed that a better person would have a better life, and that included some of the things I had asked for before. AA is okay with this view. But I no longer felt the urgency for the material things. I was starting to assume that whatever I needed would come along if I focused on being a better AA. That's the way it works. And it's much less fuss than trying to figure out what I should have and then petition for it. For example, what if you prayed for a Ferrari, got it, and then got killed in it. Wouldn't you feel silly?

There's another thing about humility that I've picked up in AA: humility is a major source of strength.

Step 8

By Step 8, I was really starting to get to know myself, and there were fewer puzzles and pirouettes in the program than in the early going. But this Step does have a poetic twist to it.

Made a list of all persons we had harmed, and became willing to make amends to them all.

Let me rewind to a conversation I had with my sponsor during Step 4. I was adding someone to my list of people who pissed me off, explaining what a jerk this person was and how richly she deserved to be on my list. I sensed agreement until my sponsor said absently, "You'll probably want to make an amend to her at some point." I wasn't sure what an amend was and my sponsor didn't object to my having her on my shit list, so I let his comment go. But I remember thinking that the chances were slim that I'd ever offer this dreadful person anything except a knife in the ribs.

At this point you're guessing, correctly, that I did end up making an amend to her, and to a number of other people on my Step 4 list. It's not so much that I came to a different view of them, as that I was able to see my part in all the messes. In Step 8, we don't necessarily try to fix broken relationships or get back to the good old days. In most cases, it's much easier than that. I just tried to figure out what would be the best possible sober relationship I could have with each person I had harmed, and I tried for that.

Wrecking relationships and blaming the other party is sport for alcoholics, and that was one reason I had become so isolated and lonely at the end of my drinking career. An honest amends list can be pretty long: family, friends, co-workers, and just about everyone I met were fair game for my antisocial talents. My sponsor pointed out that a Step 8 list should be comprehensive. The Step says "all persons we had harmed." That was a little scary to me until he added that not everyone on the list would actually be getting a hat-in-hand visit from me. In some cases, making personal amends might be hurtful to others, seriously damaging to me, or just plain crazy. The rule of common sense applies here.

In addition to being willing to ask forgiveness, being willing to forgive helped get me through Step 8. I ended up including people on my list who had harmed me too. Forgiving others made me feel a lot better, and some resentments I'd carried around for years simply vanished. Handing out a little forgiveness didn't seem unreasonable when I thought about how much forgiveness I was going to be asking for.

Step 9

Made direct amends to such people wherever possible, except when to do so would injure them or others.

Step 9 sounds easier in the abstract than it is in practice. Some AAs stare at their amends list forever, hoping for the grit to actually come face-to-face with people from their former life. I was one of those AAs. I was still deeply humiliated and ashamed of my alcoholic behavior, and the last people I wanted to chat with were those I had screwed while I was loaded. I was considering doing all my amends by e-mail.

Fortunately, divine providence intervened. One morning during my Step 9 paralysis, I got a call out of the blue from someone on my list whom I hadn't heard from in months. He asked whether I wanted to get together for breakfast. Hoping he didn't just want to slash my tires, I said yes. He'd heard that I went to rehab but knew nothing else about my journey. We had a good and frank conversation, and I awkwardly got around to my amend. Despite having lost a chunk of money thanks to me, he couldn't have been more supportive and understanding. We parted on very good terms, and I just had dinner with him this week.

Pole-vaulting over this amend left me giddy with confidence. I immediately set up an appointment with a guy who was my toughest amend to make. On game day, I dressed carefully and meditated after breakfast. I strolled into his office the picture of calm and serenity. His secretary said I looked great. In fact, all was well until the big oak door to his office swung open and there he stood. He was a little guy, but he had piercing eyes and a knack for smiling when he was giving bad news. The kind of guy I always feared. He asked a couple friendly questions like "How are you supporting yourself these days?" After a painful silence that was probably no more than a few seconds, he said, "I didn't know how far gone you were."

I felt a little strength seep into my quaking being. I started to tell my story and to explain the reason for my visit. Amazingly, he seemed to be listening with something like human sympathy. I jabbered on for double my allotted time, and he told me about an alcoholic relative that he had been supporting for years. As he showed me out, he patted me on the back and told me that he admired my courage and wished me well in my recovery. I haven't heard from him since, and that's fine for both of us.

Making amends got easier, and I liked the feeling of checking people off my list. Some amends required money to make things right; others, a sincere apology. People who lived far away got calls. Old flames got letters that I showed to my sponsor and then burned. On the subject of old flames, more than a few AAs—both women and men—have apparently used this Step as a pretext to look up former lovers. We imagine how attractive we are, all vulnerable, sober, and pure. It's a very bad idea, and a good sponsor will laugh you out of it if you're tempted.

A few people gave me the cold shoulder when I tried to make an amend. That was uncomfortable, but my job was to clean up my side of the street, so I got credit whether I got a good response or not. The rest of the people on my list were pleased to be approached honestly and seemed genuinely happy for me.

The biggest amend many of us have to make is to our spouse, that is, if our spouse has left a forwarding address. The damage we do to those closest to us is one of the tragedies of alcoholism, and the remorse that goes with it can haunt our recovery forever if we let it. There's only one solution, and that's what AAs call a "living amend." I just have to be the best sober person I can be every day from here on out. In my case, I still live with my spouse. But even if you don't, and even if you hate him or her, a living amend is the only way you'll ever put things right.

While I was working Step 9, 1 found out two things: most people believe in redemption, and redemption feels good to the redeemed.

Having worked Steps 1 through 9, I was ready for the so-called "maintenance Steps": 10, 11, and 12. I don't like the term "maintenance Steps," which sounds like an oil change. I think the final three Steps are the trifecta of sobriety and the real payoff for doing the previous nine. Steps 10, 11, and 12 showed me how to incorporate AA into my daily life as a personal code that keeps me sober and happy.

Step 10

By this point, I was starting to feel very good about life in general and about my life in particular. I wanted to keep things going that way, and Step 10 would be an important part of that. In Step 4, I made a "fearless moral inventory" of myself. Step 10 is a miniversion of Step 4. It's much less comprehensive and, once I got the hang of it, not half as hard as remembering where I parked my car used to be.

Continued to take personal inventory and when we were wrong promptly admitted it.

Threats to my newfound sobriety seem to come from two general directions: pride and complacency. This is not true for everyone, but these two seem to pop up in many AAs' sober lives. The downside of success in working the Steps can be the success itself. I have to admit that pride shaded almost everything I did in my early recovery. By the end of rehab, I was proud that I'd finally taken the plunge. I was proud of my diligence in working the Steps. I believed that I deserved the improvements in my life. I don't think any of that is really bad. As long as I realized that giving myself sole credit for my progress was nonsense, I was okay. I needed motivation to work the Steps thoroughly, and if self-satisfaction helped do the trick, so be it.

I also believe that some complacency is normal after you've completed your first run through the Steps. There was no way I could sustain the degree of emotional and intellectual focus on my recovery that I had mustered in rehab and while doing the Steps. There had to be a fifth gear, and I wanted to find it. I needed something that would keep me in continuous touch with the program without overwhelming my life. Think of the thermostat in your house: you don't look at it every ten minutes, but if you feel a little cold or a little hot, it's very useful. Step 10 is my thermostat. Here's how it works.

One day, not long after finishing the Steps (or at least my first set), I was at the gym working on the physical me. I was waiting for a piece of equipment to come open and noticed that as the previous user left, she didn't wipe it off with the antibiotic spray. There was no doubt in my mind that I was best positioned to ward off this emerging public health crisis. Confident that I was calm enough for the job, I asked her whether she planned to disinfect the equipment. She took this as an entirely inappropriate criticism of her personal hygiene and let me have it. I lost control immediately and returned fire. Both of us stormed out very upset, and the equipment remained a seething cauldron of bacteria.

I was concerned about my loss of temper, so I shared the episode with my sponsor. (By this time, I was becoming convinced that the key to effective sponsoring was an ability to nod in a wise way.) After some nodding, punctuated by raised eyebrows and a small smirk, my sponsor counseled, "Might want to try Tenth-Stepping things like this."

The advice resonated and has helped me learn to trust my instincts in two new ways. First, if I think I may have hurt another person in some way, I admit it to the injured party and try to set things right on the spot. If for some reason I can't do that, at least I accept my part in the way things went. This takes only a few minutes in most cases, and *poof*, the bad feeling's gone and I move on. Second, I'm learning to pause before responding to every little thing. I recently read about a study that showed that pauses in symphonic music stimulate a creative part of the brain—not the music, the pauses. I think that might be true. When I pause before reacting, it seems to stimulate the "don't be a jerk" lobe of my brain, and I come up with a better plan.

Bill Wilson counseled that alcoholics should probably leave righteous indignation to people who can handle it. I couldn't agree more.

Step 11

Sought through prayer and meditation to improve our conscious contact with God as we understood Him, *praying only for knowledge of His will for us and the power to carry that out.*

For me, this Step was the biggest bite of all. Taking it meant accepting a spiritual way of life that I would never have dreamed of entering. I believed in God before I started the program, and I found the Steps to be about the best self-help scheme ever. But Step 11 asked for more. I had to think about it.

I reviewed the different ways that my life had changed since I went into rehab. The news was good: I had gotten sober and healthy, and I was very happy. The people closest to me were happy too. I was integrating an appealing code of conduct into my daily life, and it suited me. I was relating to people in a relaxed and confident manner that was reassuring to me and seemed to agree with others at the same time. Maybe most important, I increasingly believed that I could sustain this new way of life for two good reasons. First, there was real depth and meaning to the AA philosophy. Second, it felt good. How in the world had all this happened to the arrogant know-it-all I was this time last year?

The answer brought me back to Step 11. I had made some

room in my life for an active relationship with a Higher Power. I admit I had done this reluctantly and skeptically. Sometimes I was afraid that it was all an illusion that would evaporate sooner or later. Sometimes I was afraid I wouldn't connect with God because I wasn't serious or worthy enough. Asking God to reveal a plan for me instead of asking for help with my plan was the biggest life change I had ever attempted. I prayed each morning for strength and guidance. I followed my prayers with meditation, hoping for answers. Even when I didn't fully believe in what I was doing, I did it anyway.

It worked.

I can't explain it, but it worked and is continuing to work in my life every day. The Steps led me to spirituality, and spirituality is now my North Star. I have gotten to know dozens of AAs who have had a similar experience. We all have one thing in common: we were afraid to rely on faith alone and demanded results.

It worked.

Step 12

I asked an AA friend with many years of sobriety what he thought was the single most important part of the program. Without any hesitation, he referred me to page 77 of the Big Book: "Our real purpose is to fit ourselves to be of maximum service to God and the people about us."

Frankly, I was hoping for something more exciting and ambitious, but I admired this oldtimer and wanted to give him the benefit of the doubt. Maybe there was more to this line than I was seeing. My answer came in Step 12.

Having had a spiritual awakening as a result of these steps, we tried to carry this message to alcoholics, and to practice these principles in all our affairs.

My friend understood that AA would have become meaningless long ago if members did not extend a hand to other alcoholics as that hand had been extended to them. As outreach programs go, AA's can seem maddeningly cautious to some of us who feel an urgency to get the word out. I admit to some frustration on this account. But alcoholism is a very personal affliction, and no mass strategy is likely to work for long. To turn my life around, I needed to talk to other alcoholics in rehab and in meetings. That's what Bill and Bob did in Akron in 1935, and that's what works today.

I find three messages in Step 12. Each is crucial to the survival of individual AAs and the survival of the fellowship.

Spiritual Awakening

AA is not about religion, but making room for spirituality in life is essential. As long as I thought I could run my life on self-will, I was condemned to a treadmill of false hope and disappointment. Accepting a Higher Power and seeking help have made the difference for me and for countless other AAs. If you don't believe it, try it. And keep trying until belief comes. It will. Step 11 sets out a simple and effective long-term strategy for building spiritual strength. Step 12 draws a bright red line under it.

Practice the Principles

You have to walk the walk for real if you expect to make it. No one gets this right all day every day. The idea in AA is to keep trying. I like this AA standby: "Do good, feel good. Do bad, feel bad. Do nothing, nothing happens." Step 10 is an effective and easy self-check on how well we're walking the walk today. Step 12 draws another bright red line here.

Carry the Message

Bill Wilson and Bob Smith believed all their AA lives that helping other alcoholics is what kept them sober. Most of the millions of AAs out there will tell you the same thing. Many of us feel a strong desire to pass it on after we've worked the Steps. I was flabbergasted by the change in my life and knew that if I could do this, so could many others. I'm no evangelist, but I wasn't about to walk around with this good news and not share it with other alcoholics who wanted to listen.

So my old friend was probably right about what's really important in AA, and Step 12 sums it up. We have to honestly stay in touch with ourselves (Step 10) and with our Higher power (Step 11). That readies us to carry the solution to others. This is AA's real bargain with us—we have to live it and share it if we expect to keep it.

Bill and Bob's final wink.

The Twelve Traditions

The Twelve Traditions are as close as AA gets to a constitution or set of bylaws, and that's not very close. To the casual observer, AA is a paradox. The fierce independence of the two Vermonters who founded it—Bill Wilson and Bob Smith—somehow forged a rabid group loyalty. I don't know anyone who can recite the Twelve Traditions, and I've seen only sporadic study of them in AA groups, compared with the constant attention routinely given to the Steps. Yet somehow many AAs seem to be familiar with the Traditions, and most of us are willing to observe their spirit at least. Here's how they work.*

Tradition 1

Our common welfare should come first; personal recovery depends upon A.A. unity.

This is more a call to the colors than an actual rule. In my experience, AAs coming into the program place their own recovery first. The unity of the fellowship is a remote concept for newcomers. That's how it was for me, anyway. It was only when I had gained some confidence in my sobriety and recognized that I couldn't have gotten sober without the group that I started thinking about unity. The "responsibility pledge" that came along in 1965 speaks more directly to this relationship between AA and the individual (see "responsibility pledge" on page 132).

Tradition 2

For our group purpose there is but one ultimate authority—a loving God as He may express Himself in our group conscience. Our leaders are but trusted servants; they do not govern.

---

* The Twelve Traditions on pages 88–95 are reprinted from *Twelve Steps and Twelve Traditions* (New York: AA World Services, Inc., 1981), 129–84.

No major religious or spiritual organization in the world cedes this kind of governing power to a spirit. Bill knew what he was doing though. He feared the political infighting that might break out when he was finally gone, but he didn't want to transfer authority to a charismatic successor. What better solution than to hand decision-making to God and execution to a servant bureaucracy? Two terms from this Tradition are heard a lot in AA: "group conscience," which translates roughly to consensus, and "trusted servants," which refers to AA's leaders after Bill and Bob and which translates to "Who are those people?"

Tradition 3

The only requirement for A.A. membership is a desire to stop drinking.

In AA's early years, each group established its own membership requirements. Some groups admitted only those who had stopped drinking and tossed out members who fell off the wagon. (As someone who initially came to AA meetings loaded, I find that a little harsh. Tipsy people need fellowship too.) Bill wrote this generous rule, and the price of AA admission suddenly became reasonable for almost anyone. If you're at a meeting and a person says, "I'm so-and-so, and I have a desire to stop drinking," you're probably dealing with someone who's curious about AA but unsure whether he or she belongs there. Or the person may be a judge, doctor, airline pilot, or someone else who may not want to admit in public to being an alcoholic. Again, hats off to Bill.

Tradition 4

Each group should be autonomous except in matters affecting other groups or A.A. as a whole.

Taking vagueness to a new frontier, Tradition 4 enjoins groups from doing anything that would bring disgrace or embarrassment upon AA and from affiliating with any other organization, such as the Catholic Church, the Republican Party, or the Hells Angels.

Tradition 5

Each group has but one primary purpose—to carry its message to the alcoholic who still suffers.

The point here is to keep AA focused on what it does well and to remind group members that we have to give it away to keep it. In other words, working with other drunks will keep us sober, and staying sober will keep us alive.

Tradition 6

An A.A. group ought never endorse, finance, or lend the A.A. name to any related facility or outside enterprise, lest problems of money, property, and prestige divert us from our primary purpose.

There is some confusion on this point among the public since the Twelve Step idea is attached to so many self-help programs around the world. AA policy is to make the Twelve

Step approach available to any person or organization. It is a kind of universal intellectual property in that sense. But AA stops short of ever offering an endorsement in the AA name—ever. Bill made most of these mistakes himself in the early AA years, so he knew what he was talking about.

Tradition 7

Every A.A. group ought to be fully self-supporting, declining outside contributions.

Bill and Bob had high hopes in the early days that America's captains of industry would rush to support AA financially. John D. Rockefeller Jr. did show some interest, but in the end, he thought truckloads of money would spoil AA. Ultimately, it was modest contributions from the groups and Big Book sales that kept AA afloat and still do today. As disappointing as it must have been when AA did not attract philanthropic support, the organization's independence today is complete, and it is unique in the nonprofit world.

Tradition 8

Alcoholics Anonymous should remain forever nonprofessional, but our service centers may employ special workers.

As AA grew, it inevitably needed a support staff. This threatened the fellowship's strict prohibition regarding making money on AA. Bill himself turned down a professional therapist job at one point in the early years when he really needed the money, so the sentiment on this ran deep. Things were settled by agreement that the Twelve Steps could not be sold in any way, but purely administrative staff could be hired to facilitate getting the message out to the still-suffering alcoholic. Today, the Twelve Step approach is freely available to other groups, and many use some version of it (Narcotics Anonymous, Gamblers Anonymous, Sex Addicts Anonymous, and so on). AA cooperates but does not affiliate. Administration of the 2-million-strong fellowship with 100,000 groups in 150 countries is handled by a professional staff of seventy-seven in New York. No comparable organization in the world runs this efficiently.

Tradition 9

A.A., as such, ought never be organized; but we may create service boards or committees directly responsible to those they serve.

Impossibly contradictory, Tradition 9 actually makes sense in the looking-glass world of AA. No one anywhere in AA can authoritatively tell anyone else in AA what to do. Members decide for themselves if they qualify as members. Groups form themselves and require no charter from a higher head-quarters. The Steps and other AA doctrine are mentored in whatever manner the mentors see fit and the students are willing to accept. AAs have agreed for many years that the fellowship should not be organized in any way. What about those "boards or committees" you might ask? In AA, these are exclusively structures that facilitate getting the message out, like the administrative staff provided for in Tradition 8. Amazingly, no one governs AA.

Tradition 10

Alcoholics Anonymous has no opinion on outside issues; hence the A.A. name ought never be drawn into public controversy.

As far as I know—and I've asked some veterans—AA has managed not to embroil itself much in the controversies about alcoholism that have percolated in the broader society over the years. Issues like temperance, the disease theory of alcoholism, federal funding for treatment, and civic initiatives like Mothers Against Drunk Driving (MADD) have been left to others, while AA remains politely on the sidelines. These topics are willingly avoided at AA meetings in favor of our focus on recovery, and this approach also governs our face to the outside world. Early AA got into a few public tar pits when members endorsed this or that, so Tradition 10 was born of experience. But AA's no-opinion policy should not be confused with know-nothing-ism. My experience with AA members is that we are as well-informed as the average person, and care as much too. In fact, caring about our fellow humans is what we do best, and that is by no means limited to other drunks.

Tradition 11

Our public relations policy is based on attraction rather than promotion; we need always maintain personal anonymity at the level of press, radio, and films.

Anonymity as an AA concept was stood on its head with the 1952 publication of this AA rule. Once again, Bill and his closest advisors had learned from their own mistakes. In the early days of AA, membership was widely viewed as a potential social and professional liability (as though being drunk all the time was not). Anyway, the original "anonymous" meant that I, as a member, could expect to keep my membership private.

Of course, AA membership is still a private matter. But with the increasing understanding of alcoholism among the general population, more and more AAs do not seem to be very tense about who knows what. The more serious concern became AAs who shouted their membership to the heavens and then fell off the wagon. The damage in those cases was not just to the individual but to AA itself. Bill came to this realization only after his own serial anonymity breaches during the 1930s and 1940s, when he went on a public speaking spree as AA's spokesman and fair-haired boy.

To his credit—and after a couple PR debacles involving AA's going public to no good end—Bill drafted Tradition 11. In my view, it comes as close to a rule as any in the lot. It is applied energetically too.

While Tradition 11 is primarily a gag order, it also sets out AA's public relations credo: "attraction rather than promotion." It clearly works, since AA has 2 million members. But some wonder whether membership would be much higher if twenty-first-century information-sharing tools were applied to getting the message out. I really don't know, nor do I sense any inclination whatever in AA to let that genie out of the bottle for now.

Tradition 12

*Anonymity is the spiritual foundation of all our traditions,
ever reminding us to place principles before personalities.*

For the spiritually tone deaf, Tradition 12 repeats the message of
Tradition 11: it's about the program, not the people! Individual
alcoholics cannot get sober if we don't protect the AA program,
even from our own best intentions. Anonymity is about much
more than not using last names or repeating things we've heard
in a meeting. It is an embodiment of the humility that is essential to recovery for all of us. Social distinctions disappear as we
walk into an AA meeting. Disaster couldn't care less where we
went to college. I think Bill and Bob got this right.

Final Word on the Traditions

Because AAs are so pigheaded, anything that looked re-
motely like a rule book is bound to be in for tough sledding.
Even today, some people view the Traditions as something
of a redheaded stepchild of the program. But we should not
sell short Bill's uncanny ability to provide for AA's long-term
growth and health, even when it went against his immediate
interests or instincts. He turned down many opportunities
to make a buck on AA over the years because he understood
that this sort of thing, if widespread, would doom the fellowship. He loved being a media darling, but he understood that
AA needed stability, not splash.

While the Traditions may be less exciting, they are as
important to the AA group as the Steps are to the individual

member. In that context, I think Bill's formulation of the Traditions was inspired. I know the Steps by heart but not the Traditions, so I remember them this way: "Please do not commercialize, professionalize, sensationalize, or personalize AA. Anything else, as long as it is good for the fellowship, is probably okay." Most of us in AA are inclined to follow the rules, since undermining the fellowship could diminish our own chances of staying sober and staying alive. Pretty good incentive.

CHAPTER 6

Spin Dry:

An Insider's Guide to AA Lingo and Slogans

Every large organization develops a unique way of communicating among its members. The lingo is usually a combination of acronyms, sayings, and inside jokes. AA is no exception, although we can't compete with major league baseball or the federal government. In fairness, not all that much of what I heard in AA, even in the very beginning, seemed to be in code. But I did have to learn some bits of jargon and AA-speak. If I heard a term that I didn't understand, I usually just asked someone around me what it meant. They'd either explain the term, tell me they weren't sure what it meant, or make something up. There is no official AA dictionary, so I'm sure I'll receive a monsoon of suggestions for improving this part of the book—and I'll be happy to do that. Think of this glossary as a well-intentioned Wikipedia entry.

Words and Phrases

AAs
Members of Alcoholics Anonymous.

Action

When I drank, I was an action-oriented person. I wanted to be where the action was. I wanted to get into the action, whatever was happening. And on Saturday nights, I was usually looking for action. Hard to believe taking action about my drinking eluded me for so long. AA fixes all that. It is above all else a program of action. Perhaps the single most important chapter in the Big Book is called "Into Action" not "Let's Think About It." We work the Steps; we don't meditate on them. There is another AA trick in all this action, in my view. While we are energetically marching through the Steps with our sponsor, the larger attraction of the program and the AA way of life is subtly showing itself to us. My sponsor says that AA looks a lot like a bootstrap program until the moment when we get a glimpse of the possibilities of actually living sober. I didn't get motivated into action in AA. It was the reverse. Tackling AA resulted in motivation. Like riding a bike—you can only get somewhere if you pedal. Conversely, if you stop pedaling, you fall. I have never been bored in AA.

Al-Anon

Originally a kind of AA auxiliary for spouses of alcoholics, Al-Anon has become the largest support group in America for the families and friends of alcoholics. Al-Anon offers insight and community for people who live with the consequences of a loved one's alcoholism. The core message in Al-Anon is "I didn't cause it, I can't control it, and I can't cure it." The answer is often "loving detachment," in which the alcoholic is cut loose to deal with the disease, although there is a lot more to Al-Anon than just this. Al-Anon can help a family member understand alcoholism and how to be supportive of the recovering alcoholic while still taking care of himself or herself. It can also open a family member's eyes to what's really going on and trigger a retreat from the relationship. Here's a good Al-Anon joke: "Any drunk can get into AA. To get into Al-Anon, you have to know somebody."

Alcoholism

Every serious medical and psychiatric association in the world subscribes to some variation of this definition from the World Health Organization:

> Alcoholism is a primary chronic disease with genetic, psycho-social and environmental factors influencing its development and manifestations. The disease is often progressive and fatal. It is characterized by continuous or periodic impaired control over drinking, preoccupation with the drug alcohol, or use of alcohol despite adverse consequences and distortions of thinking, most notably denial.

This is a long way from the "dipsomania" concept that Bill and Bob lived with in the 1930s. The point for me is that alcoholism is a recognized disease and AA is a recognized solution. What kind of screwball would choose to encourage a mortal illness rather than treat it? Hmmm. Let me think about that.

Alcohol survivor

I just don't like the word "alcoholic," so this is my preferred way of describing who we are in AA. We have a potentially fatal disease and it's in remission, so I don't see why we can't refer to ourselves as survivors. Curiously, I don't mind the word "drunk," as long as it's being used by a fellow AA and, preferably, in the past tense.

Attraction rather than promotion

You'll never receive a mailing flogging the benefits of AA membership. (Hurry while supplies last! Respect at home and at work! Serenity, courage, strength, and hope! Financial security and up to twenty-five years additional longevity!) AA has consistently resisted the temptation to seize the tools of modern media to get the word out. Fortunately, after decades of success and many news and feature articles, AA is surely the most widely known mutual support fellowship in the world. Most of us hear about AA along the way, and when we're miserable enough, we remember that it exists. That's an astonishing way to recruit 2 million members in today's world. I think more might be done to explain AA without undermining its essential person-to-person vocation, but that's my opinion only.

Big Book

This is the AA text, *Alcoholics Anonymous,* first published in 1939 and currently in its fourth edition, with sales of almost 28 million. Bill Wilson was the primary author. He was a strong proponent of calling the book *Alcoholics Anonymous* because the group had adopted that name for itself. There was competing sentiment for *The Way Out.* Bill sent an emissary to the Library of Congress to see whether either title was taken. He found nine books titled *The Way Out* and none called *Alcoholics Anonymous,* so that settled that. The reason it's called the Big Book is because in its first print run, Bill insisted that high-quality paper be used. High quality meant thick, and apparently the thing looked like a telephone book. The paper was changed in later print runs, but the name stuck. Even though it was written seventy years ago by a failed stockbroker, *Alcoholics Anonymous* is a helluva book.

Big I, little i

This is a saying you're more likely to hear in rehab than at a meeting, although I've heard it in both places. It refers to the alcoholic's two favorite personalities: the hero and the victim. "Big I," of course, is the center of attention and choreographer-in-chief. I loved this role and could never understand when others would not accept my enlightened leadership and deep understanding of whatever it was that was going on. It was a short step from there to "little i," as my attempt to control things around me failed and I became resentful. I did a lot of bouncing back and forth between hero and victim, which left me confused about which I really was. Usually, I just drank until it was clear to me that I was obviously a hero who was being treated unfairly.

Binge drinker

Some people think you can be a binge drinker without being an alcoholic. I really don't know. But alcoholism is as much about not being able to stop drinking once you start as it is about drinking often. If you're calling yourself a binge drinker to distinguish yourself from alcoholics, be careful—if it drinks like a duck, it might be a duck.

Blackout

This very spooky phenomenon causes some drunks to have a memory lapse of a couple minutes to a couple days while drinking heavily. AA meetings are full of stories of people driving five hundred miles and waking up in Vegas without a clue as to how they got there. Coming out of a binge not knowing where you went or what you did is a terrible feeling. I can remember frantically checking my pants for money and my ID, not being able to find my car, and vaguely remembering making an ass of myself. In conversations about the night before, I got good at listening for cues that might jog my memory. After one blackout, three women showed up at my house the next day, apparently at my invitation. My wife was very surprised. So was I. There are lots of people in jail who can't remember committing the crime that got them there. Blackouts are common among alcoholics, but you can still be an alcoholic and never have a blackout.

Blind faith or blind drunk

This refers to the leap we alcoholics have to make in accepting help from our Higher Power, and the possible consequences if we do not. Hard to believe, but some people choose blind drunk.

Chips

Chips look a lot like poker chips (hence the name) and are handed out at meetings to recognize sobriety anniversaries.

At my first meeting, I got something called a "desire chip." Since I was hugely insincere about AA at the time, I probably did not deserve it, although I still have it. After I got out of rehab and went back to AA, I began to collect chips at monthly intervals until I made it to a year. "Chip ceremonies" are generally quick and simple, typically coming at the beginning of a meeting. Usually the chair will ask if anyone is celebrating a "birthday." If you are, you walk up, get your chip, maybe a hug, and a round of applause. I know of one group that holds chip ceremonies only once a month and encourages recipients to say a few words. Usually, though, ceremonies are short and sweet.

The chip tradition started with Dr. Bob's inimitable nurse and longtime sidekick in the treatment of early AAs, Sister Mary Ignatia Gavin. Sister Ignatia gave patients a Sacred Heart medallion right before they finished their stay at St. Thomas Hospital in Akron, where she and Bob pioneered the treatment of alcoholics. The deal was that while patients could certainly go out and drink again if they were that crazy, they would have to return the medallion to Sister Ignatia in person before doing so. Being Irish, a nondrinker, and five-feet-two of no nonsense, Sister Ignatia was a living disincentive for potential slippers.

You are supposed to keep your chips, and some people carry them around. I have mine in a drawer in the bathroom that I open every day to get my razor. Some days I don't notice the chips lying there, but most days I do. Incidentally, at a year, the chips go from plastic to metal and seem pretty nice to me. Some long-term AAs have silver dollars with gemstones embedded for each year of sobriety that are very cool.

I suspect that this chip business sounds corny, but getting sober is so important to us that recognizing how far we've come remains important too. Chips are a useful incentive for newcomers and serve to remind all of us that we're not sober for months or years, but for a collection of individual days (see also "sobriety date" on page 135).

Cleaning up my side of the street

The Serenity Prayer asks for acceptance of the things we cannot change, and the concept of acceptance is central to success in AA. The reference to my side of the street is to the things I'm responsible for and can do something about. I've finally come to realize that I can rarely totally fix a situation if any other human being is involved. The reasonable thing is to clean up my part of the mess. Alcoholics seem to have a hard time with this, owing to an unrealistic desire to make everything right, every time. Getting used to something less satisfying but more doable is progress in our world. You'll hear this saying over and over in connection with Steps 4 and 5 and Steps 8 and 9. It's really good advice.

Closed/open meetings

You'll see meetings listed in AA schedules or on Web sites as either open or closed. Closed meetings are for those who have a desire to stop drinking, which is another way of saying AAs, since that desire is the sole criterion for AA membership. Open meetings are just that—open. AAs, Al-Anons, spouses, children, friends, and anyone else may come to open meetings. If you're still at the curious stage but ready to take a peek inside a meeting, try an open meeting. That way you have the option of introducing yourself as a visitor rather than as an alcoholic. If you don't have a schedule, you can call the local number for Alcoholics Anonymous and ask about meetings.

Contempt prior to investigation

This is the short version of a quote commonly attributed to English philosopher and political theorist Herbert Spencer (1820–1903). It's in the Big Book and is much favored by AAs to explain the danger of preconceived notions and biases as we approach the spiritual aspect of the program. Here is the full quote:

> There is a principle which is a bar against all information, which is proof against all arguments and which cannot fail to keep a man in everlasting ignorance—that principle is contempt prior to investigation. (*Alcoholics Anonymous*, 568)

I think Bill Wilson actually says it better:

> [A]ny alcoholic capable of honestly facing his problems . . . can recover, provided he does not close his mind to all spiritual concepts. He can only be defeated by an attitude of intolerance or belligerent denial. (*Alcoholics Anonymous*, 568)

Both Spencer and Wilson are talking about the first rule of intellectual honesty. You cannot reject an idea, concept, or theory that you do not understand. (Spencer himself was probably an agnostic, and so were a fair number of the original AA members.)

Cure for alcoholism

Drinking like normal people is the mirage that most alcoholics chase at one time or another and that none of us seems to reach. So there is always an audience for news stories about an alcoholism "cure." There are drugs that apparently dull the craving and one, Antabuse, that makes you deathly sick if you do drink. But alcoholism is about a lot more than just drinking, and simply not drinking won't make us whole. We drink funny partly because we think funny. Getting well means addressing both. Here is a quip that illustrates the point.

> A medical researcher comes running into an AA convention, holding a bottle of pills: "We've discovered the cure for alcoholism!" he shouts. "Just take one of these pills and your troubles will be over!" A voice from the back asks, "What happens if I take two?"

If you ask your doctor, he or she will tell you that there is no cure for alcoholism on the horizon. We can talk about treatments and remedies only. AA is hands-down the most successful.

Denial

Not that easy to define, but (like pornography) we know it when we see it. AAs can spot it immediately, because we were such masters at convincing ourselves that we weren't drunks. For a long time, I knew on some level that I didn't drink like other people, but enough things about my life were more or less normal that I could trick myself and others into thinking I was okay. As my alcoholism got worse, my denial became more frantic and less convincing. Denial is probably responsible for more life-threatening procrastination among alcoholics than anything else. I wrecked my car on a dry road at low speed without another car in sight and still convinced myself the next morning that it was only an accident. That's crazy. The opposite of denial is acceptance, and I can tell you that it feels good to make the switch.

Depression

This is a very big topic in AA. Alcohol is a chemical depressant, and most of us experienced at least some symptoms associated with depression while we were drinking. As a basically happy and optimistic person, I don't think depression led me to drink. It was probably the other way around. You may detect some disdain in AA for antidepressant medications. Since so many of us shed our depression after we stopped drinking, there is a smug feeling among some AAs that these drugs are overprescribed. But this is not a topic for the schoolteachers, engineers, sheet-rockers, and bankers in AA. If you want advice about antidepressants, ask an MD.

Drinking dreams

These dreams are weird and spooked me a lot as a newcomer. I found myself dreaming about situations in which I was about to drink, actually drinking, or already drunk. Drinking dreams were more common in the first couple months, but I still have one occasionally and veterans tell me they never entirely go away. My initial reaction was panic. I feared that I might always be haunted by booze and that the weakling in my dreams was the real me. Now if I have a drinking dream, I wake up a little upset but mostly grateful that it was only a dream and I'm sober. These dreams also remind me just how deeply drinking is wired into my brain. Maybe some AAs never have drinking dreams, but I haven't met anyone yet who has not. Drinking in my dreams is a lot better than getting up in the middle of the night for a belt, as I often did in my former life.

Drunk

I think of this word as a noun more than an adjective. I never seemed to know when I was drunk (adjective), so that would be harder to define. But I knew for a long time that I was a drunk (noun). I understand that the word grates on some people's sensibilities. I got over it, and if you're in AA for a while, you may too. Accepting that we are alcoholics is the key, and courage is the key to that acceptance. Here are a couple safety tips for using the word "drunk." First, only use it with other AAs. Second, try to use it in the past tense. Third, if someone objects, remind him or her that Bill Wilson referred to himself as a "rum hound," which is a 1930s version of a drunk. Finally, even if you just don't like the word "drunk," please don't hold it against the word "undrunk."

Drunkalog

Newcomers are encouraged at some point after joining an AA group to explain how they got there. This can be excruciating, but no one ever insists. I shared a largely made-up story when I first started going to AA. I told the real tale when I got out of rehab a few months later. Longer versions of someone's drunkalog can be heard at "speaker meetings" where members (typically those with long-term sobriety) tell their stories in some detail. Speaker meetings can be very moving and very funny. In discussion meetings, some people get too hung up on their story and seem to tell it too often. The focus of sharing in a discussion meeting is recovery; details of our past misbehavior are better left to private chats with sponsors. Regardless of what kind of story we have, it is absolutely accepted that we have all earned our chair at the AA meeting. Some AAs tell their stories at DUI programs or detox facilities as a part of their service work. You never know when your story will provide just the mirror that a newcomer needs to confront his own powerlessness and unmanageability.

Dry drunk (also called "white knuckling it")

One of my favorites. Quitting drinking is just the first step in recovery and getting sober in AA. It's the hard part and not the fun part. But getting dry is the end of the road for some alcoholics—the last stop on the "I can handle it" express. I can't imagine how hard it must be to be dry but not living sober. I'd be bitter and angry and still wanting a drink in a big way. And that's the way dry drunks are: they can't have their old life and they refuse to learn anything about a new kind of life. AA is about getting sober, staying sober, and living sober. This evolution can take you to a great place. Just getting dry is like being celibate without the peace and serenity of being a monk.

An easier, softer way

You'll hear this phrase from page 58 of the Big Book all the time in meetings. It refers to the initial reaction so many of us had to the AA program. No one's keeping score, so the temptation is strong at times to cut a corner or slide by this or that suggestion. The message is that only by taking on the program seriously and in its entirety can we expect the tremendous results so many others have had. AA is not a program of suggestions, it's a suggested program. Cherry-picking the Steps will probably not get you where you want to go. If you want to be a Marine, do the push-ups.

Emotions, instincts, and intuition

These three words live in my head and seem to have special voting rights over my behavior—sometimes for the good, other times not. I have an AA friend who misses no opportunity to remind the rest of us that almost all decisions made on the basis of emotion are bad decisions. He has a point, but love and empathy, for example, are also emotions and have places of honor in our sober lives. Instinct gets a bad rap too, since pursuing our baser ones got us into trouble as drinkers. But instincts are surely divinely given, and if we pursue them in a moral fashion, that should be okay. Intuition is my favorite of the three mystic voices. As a drinker, I was inclined to follow hunches and thought of myself as being intuitive. In reality, this was just easier than actually weighing options the way responsible people do. Since I got sober, I can distinguish between a hunch and a guess. But I'm still inclined to give intuition some weight and try to integrate it into the rest of my thought process. This is hard to describe, but I've found that some ideas that seem to enter my mind on their own can make perfect sense.

Experience versus awakening

Somewhere between the first and second editions of the Big Book (1939 and 1955), the wording of Step 12 was modified. The implication of this change was huge. The original version referred to having a "spiritual experience" as a result of the Steps, while the revised version talks about a "spiritual awakening." This goes back to Bill Wilson's "white-light experience" of suddenly being struck by divine grace or spirituality during his last stay at Towns Hospital. Bill was convinced that this epiphany was the key to his recovery and was a necessary condition for sobriety. As Bill and Bob and the other early AAs pursued their missionary work with alcoholics, they realized that white-light experiences were fairly hard to come by and that something more gradual seemed to describe the road most AAs took to spirituality. Thus, in an effort to be as inclusive as possible, the text was modified. Not everyone was happy. Father Edward Dowling, an early supporter of AA and a historic icon of the movement, said he wept at the change.

Fear

For a demographic largely defined by aggressive blowhardism, alcoholics are probably the most frightened people in your town. We are afraid of authority, obscurity, failure, success, abandonment, commitment, trust, danger, impulsiveness, being in crowds, being alone, the future, the past—get the picture? The good news (and it is incredibly good) is that working the program is the fast track to overcoming all these fears. (Remember when Dorothy threw water on the wicked witch?) It's possible to go from FEAR (f—k everything and run) to FEAR (face everything and recover).

Fifth gear

I made this up because I needed a way to express something that's very important to me in AA but that didn't have a name. What I was looking for in the program was a new way to live my life. I wanted to be sober, happy, successful, and useful to others. AA takes us in all these directions, but I needed reassurance that the program could be incorporated into my daily life without an onerous effort. I also needed to know that I would enjoy practicing my program over the long term.

I like the gear-shift analogy because I like stick-shift cars. My analogy goes like this: I sometimes have to downshift for power in tough times, and at times I have to run through the gears again to get back up to cruise speed. But when I'm on the right road and I've shifted through the gears correctly, driving is a huge pleasure. This is fifth gear. But be aware of the difference between cruising and coasting—coasting only takes you so far, and only downhill.

Five-hundred-pound telephone

Bill Wilson located his cofounder-to-be, Bob Smith, by telephone from a hotel lobby in Akron in May 1935. Ever since, a huge percentage of AA communication has taken place over the phone. E-mail plays a big role now, but there's something reassuring for us alcoholics about the voice of another drunk. However, most alcoholics are so isolated when they first come in that talking on the phone can be harder than talking with another alcoholic face-to-face. Some sponsors of newcomers suggest that their sponsees call them every day or two in the beginning. The reference to a five-hundred-pound telephone is meant to poke some good-natured fun at the newcomer who stares at the thing as if it's radioactive while she gets up the nerve to call her sponsor or another alcoholic. I had a hard time with this and thought I was pestering my sponsor. But after a while, I got used to checking in. Now I call my sponsor or other AA friends because I actually have something to say to them. Sounds almost normal, doesn't it?

Forgiveness

Most of the people from our drinking days that we'd consider forgiving have probably already forgotten what they did to us. Also, many of the wrongs of others toward us that are still festering in our early sobriety are actually things for which we bear some responsibility (see "resentment" on page 132 and "Step 4" on page 70). It might be a good idea to just get rid of this stuff. The program is great for helping us unload the rocks from our rucksack. We forgive others not to make them feel better about us, but to make *us* feel better about us.

Functional alcoholic

Whoever came up with this term should be shot. It has done more damage to the addled alcoholic than the boilermaker. The idea that I could be both an alcoholic and functional really appealed to me, especially after I started thinking

I might actually be an alcoholic. I assumed (wrongly) that many drinkers like me lived dandy lives and simply toughed out the hangovers. But what happens with functional alcoholics is that we constantly redefine downward what it means to function. Pretty soon driving home drunk without getting a DUI qualifies. One of the things I like most about AA is the emphasis on living well in the best sense. That is now my definition of functioning.

Geographic cure

The only problem with moving to another town to get a handle on your drinking is that you take yourself with you.

God

God is never defined anywhere in AA beyond "God as we understood Him" and is most often referred to in meetings as a "higher power." Since AA is scrupulously nonsectarian, mention of Jesus, Buddha, Vishnu, Zeus, and so on is frowned upon. If you must do a commercial for your personal god, you can say something like "My Higher Power, whom I choose to call Jesus . . ." I think Bill and Bob's decision to define (or not to define) God this way was a stroke of genius; it's certainly one of the reasons AA has appealed to so many different kinds of people. Some AAs who don't like the religious connotation translate GOD as good orderly direction.

God-consciousness

AA is scrupulous about not endorsing any creed. We have the concept of a Higher Power rather than God or Jesus. God-consciousness is an ancient and universal concept found in many world religions. It refers to the notion that the Higher Power, in addition to knowing and seeing all, resides within each person and works through that person. Many AAs talk about their Higher Power with casual familiarity.

God wink

Since we are encouraged to define our Higher Power however we like, I decided that mine had a sense of irony and humor. There would be no stern, judgmental, two-thousand-year-old deity for me. God winks are occurrences in daily life that we can attribute to our Higher Power, but in which he/she/it remains anonymous. They are coincidences with a twist. The most famous of these in the AA world is the chance meeting of Ebby Thacher and a totally drunk Bill Wilson, during which Ebby told Bill about getting sober through a spiritual experience. This set off the chain reaction that resulted in the establishment of AA (see "Some AA History" on page 31). The day before I "graduated" from rehab, a fellow inmate walked up to me and showed me a poem that she said was her father's favorite. I was amazed to see that it was also my mother's favorite poem and one I hadn't thought about for many years. It is attributed to the Indian poet and playwright Kālidāsa, and it is perfect for the beginner AA. It's framed on my desk and I'm looking at it as I write.

> Look to this day,
> For it is life,
> The very life of life.

In its brief course lie all
The realities and verities of existence,
The bliss of growth,
The splendor of action,
The glory of power—

For yesterday is but a dream,
And tomorrow is only a vision,
But today, well lived,
Makes every yesterday a dream of happiness
And every tomorrow a vision of hope.

Look well, therefore, to this day.

A word of caution regarding God winks: Don't get carried away looking for significance in everything that happens in your day. People will think you're squirrelly, and they'll be right.

Going out

This means a return to drinking—relapse—and is probably short for something like "going outside the fellowship and your program." Going out is the number-one bogeyman of the AA world. Thousands of AAs have gone out and come back into AA with little more than a damaged ego and a revised sobriety date, but others are not that lucky—they stay out or just disappear.

There are a couple things that scare us about someone going out. First, it often seems that the person who suddenly goes off the wagon is the one person no one thought would. We all get a little uneasy when that happens. Second, each of us wonders whether we could make it back if, for some reason, we lost our commitment to sobriety. The AA saying is "I probably have another drunk in me, but I'm not sure I have another recovery." When a member returns to AA after going out, the first question is "How did it feel?" The answer is usually that it was anything from disappointing to humiliating to terrifying. It's said that a head full of AA and a belly full of booze is a bad combination. Most people who've gone out and returned to tell the tale seem to agree that AA does ruin your drinking (see also "slip" on page 135).

HALT

HALT stands for hungry, angry, lonely, and tired. Many AAs think we should avoid these states because they're potential triggers for drinking. They are, and so are lots of other things, in my view. "Hungry" is interesting to me—like many alcoholics, I was often drinking instead of eating, which is why my bloodwork looked the way it did when I finally made it into detox. Hungry, angry, lonely, and tired all have one thing in common that spells trouble for us alcoholics: we feel vulnerable in these states and become desperate to alter our consciousness somehow. That's the real trigger.

Home group

Many AAs prefer to attend a recurring meeting because they like the people, the format suits them (open, closed, or discussion, for example), opportunities for service work are good there, and so on. In short, they feel comfortable. This is often called a home group. Mine is the noon meeting on Tuesdays at the "New Broom Group." There's no requirement to choose a home group, and even if you do settle on a preferred group for a while, you can always change your mind. Having a home group is not exclusive. I go to three or four different groups because I like the variety and I'm still getting to know AA. Something I enjoy a lot is going to a meeting while I am traveling. I always get a warm welcome, and the new setting and regional idiosyncrasies are interesting. The road can be a lonely place for AAs, so the fellowship of a meeting is not a bad idea. Also, at an out-of-town meeting, I can recycle my favorite jokes and insights without being a bore.

Hope

In AA we revere hope, probably because it was in such short supply in our previous life. Hope can sound a little weak or passive on its own, but it's mentioned at virtually every AA meeting along with experience and strength as the three qualities that all AAs share with all others.

HOW

When I first got to rehab, my memory was shot. It was like going to college on pot, which I also did. You may think memory joggers like this one are hokey, but try remembering three simple nouns sometime when you're about four days sober. HOW stands for honesty, openness, and willingness—a lot of AAs think these three are the keys to success in working through the Twelve Steps. I do too.

Hugs

My in-laws are Latino, and everybody hugs everybody all the time. That took some getting used to at first. But AA takes hugging to the next level. We hug each other before meetings and after meetings. If someone gets upset during a meeting, here comes a hug. Trying to fend off an incoming hug with an extended handshake is probably not going to work. I decided that extreme measures would be required if I were to maintain my dignity amid all this hugging. So I just started hugging everyone too. For what it's worth, I think AA hugs are more genuine than, say, the hugs on *The Sopranos*. If you're a newcomer, at least try hugging—you may like it. If you're a boy and you're hugging a girl and your hip bones are touching, you're probably overdoing it.

Humility versus humiliation

I have heard that humility is a clear understanding of who and what we are and an honest desire to be something better. Humiliation is recognition that another person sees you as defective, guilt-ridden, and shameful. In AA, humility is sought because it is essential to place us in the proper relationship with our Higher Power and with others. Humiliation is something most alcoholics are pretty familiar with, but it doesn't lead to humility. It just leads to low self-esteem and usually more drinking.

Impulsiveness

This means what you think it means, but somehow we alcoholics manage to turn a common human foible into a tragic-comic art form. So much of what I did drunk that I truly regret was a direct result of impulsiveness. The think-say-do chain in a drunk knows no speed limits and often results in buffoonery and bad behavior. In sobriety, AAs have to be especially watchful of this old enemy, lest it put a drink in our hands before we know what's going on.

Jack Alexander article

In March 1941, an article about AA appeared in *The Saturday Evening Post* that introduced the fellowship to a national audience for the first time. Jack Alexander was the reporter who wrote it. As a direct result of the publicity, sales of *Alcoholics Anonymous* soared and membership around the country took off. This was the break Bill and Bob had been seeking for six years, and AA has been part of the national vocabulary ever since. Alexander later served as a nonalcoholic trustee of AA, and the article is available in a pamphlet from AA World Services. To his credit, Alexander got the gist of AA mostly right, although he referred to us as "inebriates." The article is often cited within AA as proof that there's no need to advertise the fellowship. The conventional wisdom is that the word will just get out. That would have been little comfort to the alcoholics who went down the tubes while the *Post* was getting around to publishing an article.

Carl Jung

Carl Jung (1875–1961) was a Swiss psychiatrist and founder of analytical psychology. Bill Wilson credited him with having an important influence in AA's conception of spirituality. Through a remarkable chain of events in the 1930s, Jung's advice to an American alcoholic that a spiritual experience was his only chance at recovery reached Bill in New York at a particularly low point in his own disease. Bill attributed his "white-light experience" to the power of this message. He finally exchanged letters with Jung in 1961, telling him the story of the profound impact the message had on the development of AA. Jung's response confirmed Bill's understanding of what the psychiatrist had meant: drinking was a kind of spiritual quest. Jung said, "[The alcoholic's] craving for alcohol was the equivalent on a low level of the spiritual thirst of our being for wholeness, expressed in medieval language: the union with God." Jung agreed with Bill that true spirituality played a role in recovery.

The legacies

In 1955, when Bill Wilson declared AA to be organizationally mature and able to run itself, he identified three legacies as pillars of the fellowship. The legacies are recovery (the Twelve Steps), unity (the Twelve Traditions), and service (the administrative structure that supports AA as an organization without governing it). Bob Smith had died in 1950, and Bill recognized the need to set AA on a self-sustaining course into the future that was independent of any personalities—including his own. AA would belong to the members, and the legacies would ensure that. AA owes its long-term survival to Bill Wilson's humility and foresight (see "Some AA History" on page 31).

Making amends

"Oh," I thought, "I have plenty of experience with this." In Step 8 we make a list of people we hurt while drinking; in Step 9 we make amends to them. These amends are different from the budzillion apologies and promises of better behavior I was familiar with. AA amends are meant to clean our house. If there is a positive effect on the injured party, great, but that's not why we make amends. I carried the harm I had done to others around like a bag of rocks. As I made amends, I was able to empty the bag, one rock at a time. I was scared to see some of the people on my list, but I was amazed at how many were understanding and even expressed admiration for what I was doing. Some still hated me and saw my amend-making as proof that I was a beaten person. I didn't care once I understood that this was for *my* recovery. Lots of AAs procrastinate on making amends, and I did some of that myself. Let me tell you, though, it's a great experience once you get going. Oh, yes—Step 9 is not an excuse to look up old lovers. AA makes it clear that some amends are best made by simply leaving the injured party alone.

Marijuana maintenance program

This is a favorite mirage of sobriety for AAs from teens to boomers. "I'm not drinking, so I must be okay" is the motto of any maintenance program that involves another drug such as marijuana, Ecstasy, Valium, or OxyContin. I haven't seen it work, and I hear from AAs who've given it a whirl that it doesn't work (see "pills count" on page 127).

The musts

Bill Wilson wrote the Big Book, but the drafting process was characterized by ongoing review by the New York and Akron AA groups, as well as by trusted nonalcoholic experts and friends of AA. When the final manuscript was ready, Bill circulated four hundred mimeographed copies for comment, just to be sure he was still on the right track. One of the criticisms was that there were too many "musts" in the text that probably should be changed to "shoulds." Bill made many changes, but quite a few "musts" survived. They tend to focus on the more important elements of the program—like the demons of self-will, resentment, and procrastination—as well as the positive effects of faith, amends, and spirituality. Even though the founders were sure they had the solution to alcoholism, Bill toned the manuscript down enough to call the Twelve Steps a suggested program of recovery.

Narcotics Anonymous

There are dozens of "anonymous" movements around the country (Gamblers Anonymous, Sex Addicts Anonymous, and so on). AA endorses none but cooperates with all by making its Twelve Step program freely available. I mention NA because it's the one we see most of in AA. It's no surprise that many NAs are hooked on alcohol too. There's some blowback from traditionalist AAs that addicts don't belong in AA. NAs, on the other hand, believe that alcohol is just another drug and welcome AAs to their meetings. You can decide for yourself how to feel about this divide, which seems like a nonissue to me.

Newcomer

There is no set criterion for newcomer status. I think of newcomers as AAs with fewer than ninety days of sobriety. Veteran AAs tend to watch out for newcomers and cut them a lot of slack in those confusing early days. The presence of newcomers is AA's most tangible sign of institutional health.

Sometimes there's an element of fraternity or sorority rush in getting to know them, but most AAs recognize newcomers' need for space as they scope out the group and its dynamics. All of us have been there, so there's widespread sympathy for the drama of finally coming to AA. In better meetings, an experienced AA will typically buttonhole a newcomer afterward to add a personal welcome, often giving out his phone number and a few words of encouragement. Sometimes, though, the newbie makes a break for the door so fast that there is no opportunity. In those cases, we can only hope our newcomer will have heard something that makes him or her want to come back.

Ninety and ninety

Newcomers are encouraged to attend ninety AA meetings in their first ninety days of sobriety. When I first heard this, I almost laughed out loud. I was busy, after all, and such frantic repetition seemed absolutely desperate to me. I was wrong. A ninety-and-ninety approach may be the best insurance a newcomer can buy to stay sober in the crucial early going. A busy meeting schedule helped me as a newcomer resist the craving and get more comfortable with the support the group offers. AA friends who did not go to rehab have told me that their ninety and ninety launched them into sobriety. After I started going to meetings regularly, I quickly stopped counting because I enjoyed them so much. By the way, if you think going to AA meetings takes up too much of your time, do the math on how much time you spent stockpiling booze, drinking it, and recovering from hangovers in your old life. You'll faint.

Normies

Normal people. People who can have a drink or two and stop. Nonalcoholics. Early in his first administration, Ronald Reagan was at an embassy reception in Washington, D.C. He had an empty cocktail glass in his hand. The waiter asked him if he wanted another drink. "Why would I want a drink?" the president said. "I just had one." This is the normal drinker that all alcoholics yearn to be (as long as it means drinking as much as we want) and that none of us ever will be.

Oldtimer

There's no official threshold for oldtimer status, but ten to fifteen years of sobriety seems to be generally accepted. When I first came in, that seemed like a hundred years. It still seems like a long time. Oldtimers play a unique role in AA. They're the institutional memory and often the conscience of a group, but rarely are they the day-to-day leaders, although most of them probably were earlier in their sobriety. Oldtimers in AA benefit from an almost Asian reverence for their wisdom and insight. And yet, ask any oldtimer and he or she will tell you it's still one day at a time. Surprisingly few oldtimers seem to use AA as a social life surrogate. If we add square dancing at meetings, that could change.

Oxford Group

The Oxford Group was an early twentieth-century American evangelical movement, founded by Lutheran minister Frank Buchman in the 1920s, that had a major influence on the genesis of AA. The spiritual component of recovery was first explained to Bill Wilson by his friend Ebby Thacher, who was an Oxford Group member. Early AAs met with Oxford Group members, although alcoholism was always incidental to the Oxford agenda. The Oxford Group renamed itself "Moral Re-Armament" in 1938, adopting an institutional focus on world peace. AA went its own way in the late 1930s, when the Akron and New York groups separated entirely from the Oxford Group organization. Bill Wilson had a gift for idea theft, and he looted the Oxford intellectual treasury shamelessly. Inspiration for the Steps came from the Oxford teachings, and AA borrowed the small-group meeting format and person-to-person communication concept from Oxford. Bill also had a sixth sense about what made AA unique and what needed to be done to build an enduring organization that could help alcoholics many years into the future. That particular genius was my good fortune and has been the good fortune of millions of other alcoholics who have gotten sober in AA.

Paralysis by analysis

The AA founders did not have much time for science or medicine, maybe because both had let them down so completely. The first AAs got sober by sticking together, working their programs, and spreading the AA message to those who needed to hear it. This saying endorses Bob Smith's advice to "keep it simple" and the Big Book's emphasis on action, not contemplation. Most of us can't afford psychoanalysis, so this may be a worthwhile approach to getting well.

People-pleaser

Many alcoholics seem to fall into indiscriminate people-pleasing to feel accepted and boost their self-esteem. That's

the conventional wisdom anyway. People-pleasing is the opposite of having sincere concern for others and being a better person yourself. That's conventional wisdom too. I was a
people-pleaser, and I can spot one at a hundred yards.

Picking up

This means having a drink. I've never heard anyone outside
of AA refer to having a drink as picking up a drink. But the
visual image of picking up a drink is a powerful one for us.
It's more like spinning the cylinder on a pistol in a game of
Russian roulette than proposing a toast at a wedding. I was
confused the first few times people told me that all I had to
do to stay sober was "not pick up." Now I say the same thing
to newcomers.

Pills count

I think mood-altering drugs taken primarily to alter your
mood are no different than vodka taken to alter your mood.
Not everyone agrees, especially people who take pharmaceu-
ticals in place of booze and consider themselves to be sober.
Taking sedatives to dull the shakes is an old trick ("Doctor,
Alcoholic, Addict," in the third edition of the Big Book, is a
good story in this connection). Modern-day alcoholics—ever
on the lookout for innovation—have moved into the opiate-
barbiturate arena, tossing back OxyContin, Vicodin, Xanax,
and others to ease their pain. When I asked one oldtimer why
pills are such a phenomenon, he gave me a you're-not-too-
bright look and said, "Can't smell 'em." Some AA purists will
tell you that drug problems belong in drug-focused recovery groups like Narcotics Anonymous. At the AA meetings

I go to, many attendees introduce themselves as "alcoholic-addicts." You'll have to decide for yourself about pills, but I'm convinced that mother's little helper can really be a mother. This doesn't apply to nonaddictive medications prescribed by an MD for a diagnosed disorder, of course.

Pink cloud

This refers to the strong and abiding feelings of joy and optimism that characterize early sobriety for most of us. Some people say this peacefulness is God's grace entering our lives. Others say it comes from a renewed connection with the people and the world around us. Curmudgeons say that anyone who drank the way we did and quit *should* feel great. I think it's a combination of all three. Most people agree that the pink cloud is temporary; it's hard to sustain that kind of near-ecstasy. Still, being sober and working my AA program has upped my joy quotient by a lot. I get a couple glimpses of the pink cloud every day. Don't be bashful about embracing the pink cloud. If you feel it, it's real. If anyone snickers at your ebullience and occasional fits of public happiness, feel free to ignore that person.

Principles before personalities

In 1955, AA formally rejected an organizational concept based on charismatic leadership or big-name members and sponsors. From 1935 to 1950, AA had been a two-man show run by Bill Wilson and Bob Smith. Bill was the visionary of AA and Bob the conscience (see "Some AA History" on page 31). But as they aged and as Bob's health faltered, they realized that they would have to either pass the reins to a new generation of star-leaders or create a nameless, faceless governing structure to replace themselves. They opted for the latter, and the "trusted servant" model of government has been just right for AA ever since. I really appreciate this minimalist leadership model because it neutralizes my unfortunate tendency to want to dominate any group I join. And I'm not alone in this—the percentage of alphas sitting around any AA meeting table can't be explained by probability. The fact that we remain on such good behavior is beyond modern psychology. I think it's because our lives depend on those meetings.

Progress, not perfection

This comes from the Big Book, and you'll hear it over and over in AA. It goes to the heart of the alcoholic's warring instincts toward control and perfectionism on one hand and low self-esteem on the other. "Progress, not perfection" is meant to reassure us that the grading curve for our recovery will be charitable as long as we're moving in the right direction. Becoming a better person every day—even if only a little better—sustains many AAs over the long term and, when you think about it, is a pretty good way to live.

Proof

This refers to the alcohol content of everything from beer and wine to Bacardi 151. Proof is controlled by governments around the world to protect consumers, although some, like alcoholics, are out of control and don't care. For me, the proof on a bottle was helpful only insofar as it told me how many I'd have to buy. It was a different kind of proof that unlocked AA for me. I needed proof that the program would work as advertised. I didn't get this all in one revelation but in moments of affirmation as I went along. I was a skeptic because I'd been sold the Brooklyn Bridge a few times in my drinking life. And look how much proof of my drinking disease I required before I believed that anything was seriously wrong!

Queer mental condition

This bit of vintage 1930s English from page 92 of the Big Book means roughly "brain cramp." I wish I had a dollar for every time I vowed not to have a drink and did. Most times, I told myself I'd just have a couple. Later in my drinking career, I told myself I would commence moderation tomorrow. Later still, I just said, "Screw it." Whatever the self-delusion, I ended up drinking a lot. I believe that all alcoholics suffer from this mental condition to one degree or another. It may be the primary behavioral marker of our type. We cannot safely drink because we are unable to have just a couple without having a couple more. The Big Book, on page 33, also calls this unfortunate turn of mind a "mental twist."

Raising the bottom

This refers to the evolution of AA from 1939 to about 1955 and its growing willingness to work with drunks who were not terminal. Early AAs believed that only real down-and-outers would have the motivation to succeed in the program. That turned out not to be true, and AA's communal heart began reaching out to drunks whose lives did not yet look like something out of Dickens. Personally, I believe that one has to experience some serious pain to be a good candidate for AA. It's hard to see the wisdom of the program from the comfort of a pre-disaster life. But I'm grateful for the generosity of the early AAs in letting drunks at all stages benefit from this incredible option.

Rehabilitation (rehab, spin dry)

This is where movie stars, athletes, and politicians go. If you're lucky and still have health insurance, you might go there too. Rehab is usually four weeks, and the treatment approaches vary. I think Twelve Step programs are the best treatment option out there. I remember during my first couple days of rehab, I overheard a woman who was finishing up say that she wasn't sure she was ready to leave. I thought, *Are you crazy? Give me your release papers!* Later, I got to the point where I actually liked my rehab facility. More important, I liked what I was getting out of it. But I never wanted to stay an extra minute, and I only want to come back for alumni events.

As I look back on it, rehab was absolutely crucial to jumpstarting my recovery. I needed some time in relative isolation to think things through, and the company of other drunks was extremely important (fellow inmates, for sure, but many counselors are also recovering alcoholics). They say one month of rehab is equal to six months of meetings. I don't know, but it's worth a lot if you settle in and give it a chance. Also, I made some genuine friends inside. Some have stayed sober, but others have not. Not everyone in AA gets there via rehab, but quite a few do. Some go more than once, and some seem to be going in and out for years. If you can afford it or have insurance or other coverage, I recommend one honest shot at rehab. If that doesn't take, go again.

Rehab is discovery and AA is recovery, so they say, and I believe it.

Resentment

Bill Wilson generally steered clear of categorical statements or explicit warnings in the Big Book, preferring to let us figure most things out for ourselves. But he made an exception for resentment, about which the Big Book (page 64) says, "Resentment is the 'number one' offender. It destroys more alcoholics than anything else." I'm absolutely convinced he was right. There was something hardwired into my brain that triggered resentment all day long. From traffic to the state of the world, I was more or less continuously miffed about something. Drinking tamed the dragons inside me, but only for a time. Like most alcoholics, I was an expert at justifying my resentments: "He cut me off in traffic." "I should have gotten that promotion." "The president is ruining the country." My resentments were mostly stuff that I either played a negative role in (I didn't get the promotion because I drank on the job) or things that were beyond my control (the president doesn't know me or care what I think). Resentment can slip into our lives anytime we let our guard down. The good news is that AA helps me quickly recognize a resentment as something I'm at least partly responsible for or have no control over, so I can toss it overboard on the spot. Getting in a sweat over resentment is a lot like drinking poison and hoping the other person will die.

Responsibility pledge

Consider this: a couple million alcoholics take an oath to be responsible for making AA recovery unconditionally available to millions more alcoholics around the world. Skeptical? I couldn't even be responsible for making sure I didn't run out of vodka when that was my top priority. If I add the words "or I will die" to the spirit of the pledge, it seems to make a difference. Here is the AA responsibility pledge, adopted in 1965:

> I am responsible. When anyone, anywhere, reaches out for help, I want the hand of AA always to be there. And for that: I am responsible.

The pledge goes to the heart of the AA philosophy. We are individually responsible for our own recovery, but we are responsible as a group for everyone else's. When someone in trouble looks up Alcoholics Anonymous in the phone book, an AA will answer the phone. When someone who is ready to try a meeting checks the schedule on the Internet, those meetings will be held at those locations. When someone needs a sponsor, a sponsor will come forward. When a member is in crisis, AAs will make a Twelfth Step call. One of the cornerstones of our movement is that no AA can be assured of keeping his sobriety unless he is simultaneously willing to carry the AA message to other alcoholics. This is a big incentive toward responsibility.

The rooms

This refers to AA meetings. Why they're called the rooms is a mystery to me, but you're likely to hear it from someone at a meeting. Maybe it sounds more profound to say "when I first came to the rooms" rather than "at my first meeting." I used it more as a newcomer than I do today. Not that that means anything.

Serenity Prayer

Early in sobriety, I was chatting about AA with my sister, who has twenty-five years in the program. She said, "You know, the Serenity Prayer pretty much says it for me." I hadn't really given the prayer much serious thought, even though it's recited at virtually every AA meeting around the world. Since then, though, I've come to agree that you couldn't get or give better daily advice than that found in the Serenity Prayer, which is attributed to Reinhold Niebuhr (1892–1971). I go to one meeting at which the chairman always says before we recite the prayer, "Now let's all really think about the words." More good advice.

> God, grant me the serenity to accept the things I cannot change, the courage to change the things I can, and the wisdom to know the difference.

A fellow AA gave me the prayer on a key-chain medallion that I always carry. I like that.

Show up and grow up

Almost every self-help or counseling program talks about growth, and AA is no exception, but we see it from a slightly different perspective. I drank through my twenties and thirties, and it seems that many other AAs did too. For me, those years were marked by a decided absence of maturing. I thought in my drinking days that I was just blessed with a fun-loving personality and that people around me were impressed that someone with my responsibilities could be so lighthearted and even frivolous at times. The truth was that I was just a drunk who hadn't grown up. The darker side of alcoholic immaturity includes financial irresponsibility, risky behavior, and impulsiveness. AA recognizes and forgives this. Getting sober is a terrific crash course in maturity. I can't believe how great it feels to be an adult at last.

Slip

A slip is when an alcoholic who has abstained for some period of time goes back to drinking or drugging. A slip can last the time it takes to down a shot or it can last the rest of your life. It is typically a very emotional experience for the alcoholic, who presumably wanted to stop drinking. An AA can come back into the fellowship anytime after a slip, and he or she will be warmly welcomed. No one thinks that a slip erases sober time, although sobriety dates are adjusted and the clock starts over again. There are as many reasons for slips as there are alcoholics who slip. One popular explanation is that the alcoholic stopped working the program or stopped coming to meetings. Another is that the alcoholic was just not ready to quit. One old standby holds that SLIP stands for sobriety lost its priority. I haven't slipped, so my knowledge is secondhand. But I will say that slips by friends in the fellowship remind the rest of us just how cunning, baffling, and powerful the disease of alcoholism really is (see also "going out" on page 116).

Sobriety date

Not dinner and a movie with another AA. We all keep track of the time we have sober in the program, and the date of our last drink is called our sobriety date. Very cheesy aluminum coins or poker chips are given to members at meetings on their first day, and at one month, three months, and six months sober. When you reach one year, the coins get a little nicer and are handed out at one-year anniversaries thereafter. These are quick no-frills ceremonies at meetings, but everyone applauds and you may be asked by the chairman to share your wisdom. I thought the sobriety date was a corny tradition at first. *This isn't Weight Watchers,* I'd complain to myself. But I've come around on the subject. The day of my last drink was a momentous occasion in my life, and not recognizing that risks diminishing the decision I made that day. I'm convinced that AA gave me one of life's precious second chances, and that's an anniversary worth remembering. Since I know how many years it's been since the Cubs won the pennant and how long ago I graduated from high school, surely I can recall how long AA and I have held alcoholism at bay. This is about life and death, isn't it? (See also "chips" on page 102.)

Spiritus contra spiritum

Bill Wilson attributed his jump start in recovery to the "white-light experience" he had at Towns Hospital during his last rehab stay in 1934. He became convinced that only such an experience could bring alcoholism to remission. Through a chain of events (see "Some AA History" on page 31), Bill ended up corresponding in 1961 with Swiss psychiatrist Carl Jung (see page 120), who agreed on the importance of the spiritual component to defeat alcoholism. Jung referred to *spiritus contra spiritum* (the spirit against spirits). Bill took this as validation from a top authority for his own theory of recovery. In AA practice, however, no white-light experience is considered necessary, and the Twelfth Step refers only to a "spiritual awakening." I've met some AAs who had big-bang experiences and others who've come to personal spirituality more gradually. Both types seem to have an equal shot at recovery. Most of AA is not this complicated, but spirituality is worth working to understand, in my view (see "Spirituality" on page 36).

Stinkin' thinkin'

You'll hear this a lot in AA. It refers to the peculiar turn of mind we alcoholics have in the way we think about people, places, and things around us. I overrated myself, yet I was constantly fearful. I blamed others for much of what I had caused myself. I was very good at spinning out daydreams and conversations in which my wit or courage triumphed, but I had a hard time actually getting things done. Alcoholics are not the only folks who can think ourselves into a hole, but we do seem to have a gift for it.

I'll never forget my second day in rehab, going in to breakfast for the first time and seeing other inmates wearing cardboard signs: "Ask what I'm grateful for," "I am a worthwhile person," and so on. One guy was carrying a bag of rocks around and asking people to help him get rid of them by taking one. Another person was wearing a blindfold and being led around. This was Dante's third circle of hell as far as I was concerned. The worst humiliation by far, in my terrified opinion, was the woman wearing a skunk-skin hat and a cardboard sign that said "Stinkin' Thinkin." I had one friend (my roommate, who was also new), and we made a do-or-die pledge that we would never, ever wear any of that silly, degrading stuff. (If you were thinking about rehab but are now having second thoughts, relax. This isn't necessarily standard practice in treatment programs.)

It turns out that stinkin' thinkin' is a very important AA concept. In addition to being physically addicted to alcohol and unable to normally process it in our alcoholic brains, we are also self-centered, self-pitying, controlling, out of control, negative, falsely saccharine, paranoid, arrogant, delusional, timid, grandiose, and pessimistic in measures well beyond the norm. This is our peculiar mental condition and something that will need our attention in recovery long after the urge for a cold one has become history.

Incidentally, I wore both the blindfold (I had trust issues) and the skunk hat before I graduated. Amazingly, I thought of both as important learning experiences. Guess I showed them.

Taking my own inventory

AAs take more inventory than the Ford Motor Company. What this refers to is the practice of reviewing daily, or even moment to moment if necessary, our thinking and behavior to see if it's healthy. It is related to the Tenth Step: "Continued to take personal inventory and when we were wrong promptly admitted it." For example, your Saturday newspaper is not delivered and so you don't know which college football games will be on TV. You call the paper and let the woman in circulation have it. But she does not actually deliver the paper, and you could look up the games online. By apologizing to her, you make her feel better (or less bad), admit to yourself that you were wrong, and emerge stronger and in a better frame of mind altogether. This sounded a little cumbersome and neurotic to me at first but, as with so much in AA, there's a trick: after going through this self-awareness ritual a few times, I stopped making some of the rude remarks or out-of-proportion responses in the first place.

Taking someone else's inventory

Measuring other people against some impossible standard is an alcoholic pastime. It played right into my self-centeredness and fake self-confidence. It's also a hard habit to break. I heard a guy in a meeting once say that you'd know you were really recovering the first time you stood in line at the grocery store and didn't take everyone's inventory. AA is all about fixing ourselves and being charitable toward others, which is the opposite of how I thought for most of my adult life.

Terminally unique

This refers to the self-centeredness that can keep us away from AA altogether or slow us down once we're inside and giving it a try. Symptoms of being one of the chosen few can be pretty funny: (1) We probably do not belong in AA. (2) We are too smart and successful to be in the same room with all these losers. (3) Our story is the saddest story we have ever heard.

Of course, I'm far from unique, and the longer I hang around meetings, the clearer that becomes. The good news is that our strength in AA lies in our common ground, and that's where we find recovery too. I know that "unique" is a stand-alone word that requires no modifier. But as we dither with our specialness, our disease advances relentlessly. That's where "terminally" fits in.

Thirteenth-Stepping

There is no Thirteenth Step, so be careful of this one. Thirteenth-Stepping is making a romantic move on a fellow AA, especially a newcomer. "So what?" you might say. Well, many AAs are vulnerable, and the combination of wrecked lives, new hope, and new people can make for a heady atmosphere. Also, AA encourages bonding, sharing, and candor on a level not found in other open groups. Women are sometimes looking for love and men for companionship. For that reason, sponsors usually keep an eye on newcomers and generally suggest that they get a year in the program before making any big moves in their lives. While there are opportunists out there, I think most AAs are at least as careful as the average person about relationships. Maybe more careful, having wrecked most of our former relationships while drinking. Here's an old joke that's popular among British AAs: "If you're looking for romance in AA, the odds are good. Trouble is, the goods are odd."

Trigger

A trigger is anything that makes you want to have a drink. For alcoholics, that could be anything and everything. I had a counselor who told me that he helped a woman who felt the need for vodka every time the wind changed direction. I think he was kidding. Triggers can be things like passing the bar where you and your boyfriend used to hang out or stopping by the clubhouse after a great (or miserable) eighteen holes. As a newcomer, I found it useful to think about what made me want to have a drink. Heightened awareness is a good thing, but the demon can ambush me at any time, so it's what I do with the urge that counts.

Trusted close-mouthed friend

By the time most of us get to AA, we are pretty well isolated and having problems trusting others. That's not good. Opening up with a sponsor is part of the road back from our sorry state. But a sponsor, at least initially, will want to maintain a mentoring relationship, which includes some distance. This is where a trusted close-mouthed friend comes in. The cornerstone of AA is that we cannot recover alone; building confident relationships is crucial. It is especially important to choose well in the beginning. This special friend can be a counselor, a member of the clergy, or just a trusted friend. An old drinking buddy is probably not the right choice. I don't know why they call these people "trusted close-mouthed friends," unless maybe it's to let us recovering alcoholics demonstrate our new control over speech.

Twelfth Step call

A cross between a doctor's house call and a SWAT team assault, a Twelfth Step call is serious business and not for amateurs. Typically, an alcoholic who has gotten drunk or thinks drinking is imminent qualifies for a call. Sometimes he contacts his sponsor; sometimes his sponsor has a bad feeling and contacts him; sometimes a family member or friend raises the alarm. The purpose of a Twelfth Step call is to be present for the suffering alcoholic, to encourage him either not to drink or not to continue drinking. The idea is to limit the damage to all concerned as the drama of the alcoholic fighting with his addiction plays out. Twelfth Step calls are not made alone because there's always the chance that a one-person rescue party might decide to join the drinker.

If things get hairy, police or medical professionals are called in. Ideally, a very experienced AA unofficially leads the delegation. Newcomers can be brought along for on-the-job training. Twelfth Step calls are not the same as interventions, which are typically more choreographed and usually undertaken according to timing determined by the family and friends of an alcoholic. Most Twelfth Step calls take place between 1:00 a.m. and 3:00 a.m., or whenever you're doing something important or enjoyable. AAs do not duck Twelfth Step calls.

Undrunk

For the purposes of this book, "undrunk" means living the AA recovery program. Undrunk does not mean that our alcoholism is cured, but it means that we are beating the hell out of its major symptoms, like drinking our heads off, thinking with the clarity of a gerbil, racking up as many character defects as possible, leading what can only charitably be called a troubled life, and waging all-out war on our internal organs. Undrunk is probably an adjective, but it could be a noun too.

The yets

I heard this often as a newcomer. To differentiate myself from "hardcore" alcoholics, I'd point out in meetings that I hadn't lost my house or my wife or my job, nor had I gone to prison or been shot or stabbed. This kind of hair-splitting is not unusual among newcomers. It's partly denial that we are alcoholics at all and partly insistence that, although we may be alcoholics, we're not really *bad* alcoholics. The response from experienced AAs is usually a kindly "not yet." The point is that it doesn't matter where we happen to be in alcoholism's game of Chutes and Ladders, we're all heading toward the same rotten place. Understanding this is essential to acceptance, which, in turn, is essential to everything else. Some people say YET stands for you're eligible too.

Sayings

AA is a simple program for complicated people.

Bill Wilson and Bob Smith were careful about keeping the AA program simple. In fact, Bob's last words to Bill were "Let's not louse this thing up. Let's keep it simple." There are few rules, minimal government, and a concise and unambiguous program of action. But add alcoholics to the mix and just see how complex it can get. Some alcoholics will inevitably overanalyze the Steps, try to control the meetings and change the structure, enforce rules disguised as norms, and do whatever else they can to turn a simple Greek structure into a rococo palace. Fortunately, AA groups seem to have a natural self-correcting capacity that kicks in whenever efforts to "improve" the program get up a head of steam.

AA is not bad people trying to become good,
but sick people trying to get well.

Because of the acceptance of the disease theory of alcoholism by all major medical and psychiatric associations—including the American Medical Association and the World Health Organization—more and more people understand that alcoholism is a genetically transmitted progressive illness. But stigmas die hard, and many folks, including some MDs and shrinks, still think there's a willpower deficit at work here. I live with it and so will you. The good news is that most people recognize success when they see it, and AAs are successful. So many people are touched by alcoholism directly or indirectly in the United States and around the world that the example of AA's powerful effect comes as a welcome hope to millions.

All of us together know more than any one of us.

I think AAs are smarter than the general population, and it's a safe bet that AAs in general agree. That can make for interesting meetings. The downside is that some of us will inevitably try to dazzle the rest from time to time. This tried-and-true saying is a call to humility and a reminder of the reality that no one in the room is really smarter than everyone else put together. I wish Congress ran this way.

Bring the body and the mind will follow.

This saying was probably lifted from somewhere else, but in AA, it refers to the benefit of repeatedly coming to meetings, paying attention (even if you don't exactly understand what it's all about), and trusting that a light will eventually come on. It will. Bill Wilson was smitten by American psychologist and philosopher William James's book *The Varieties of Religious Experience,* which he read in Towns Hospital. James (1842–1910) talks about "acting yourself into a new way of thinking," and this got Bill's attention. The Big Book chapter "A Vision for You" evokes the concept of acting yourself into a new person. That's partly why AAs always tell newcomers to "keep coming back" to meetings and why, at the end of meetings, they say, "It works if you work it." AA slang for this concept is "fake it 'til you make it," and many people do just that.

Continue doing what you're doing and you'll keep getting what you've got.

Conventional AA wisdom is that the definition of insanity is doing the same thing over and over and expecting a different result. That's what my life was all about. This saying is a shot over the bow on the need for acceptance. We have a problem, and we need to take some decisive action to fix ourselves.

Do good, feel good. Do bad, feel bad. Do nothing, nothing happens.

This saying is an AA standby. I have an Italian friend who says it with a Cosa Nostra delivery that makes everyone want to believe it. I believe it.

Don't drink, go to meetings, work the Steps.

This is fabulously good advice, and newcomers hear it all the time. It comes in handy for veteran AAs too. Winston Churchill said famously that in difficult times, always return to "first principles." It was during World War II, and he was referring to things like courage and patriotism. I think the saying could also apply to AA. Getting sober, staying sober, and living sober is a big job, and we all get overwhelmed from time to time. For some of us, the answer is more meetings. For others, a call to our sponsor, some reading in the Big Book, or some service work does the trick. For all of us, it's about not drinking no matter how rocky things get.

Don't quit before the miracle happens.

This refers to the idea that repeated exposure to AA will sooner or later result in comprehension of the message, embrace of the principles, and the miracle of recovery. In this sense, it's a variation on "keep coming back." I've never heard of anyone who "got" AA at their first meeting. Most people are at least a little uncomfortable in the beginning, and AA probably scares more than a few away. Resisting the urge to run from AA pays off before too long.

Don't think less of yourself. Just think of yourself less.

When I came into AA, I was all mixed up about the most important topic in my life: me. On the one hand, I thought I was the most gifted person I knew. On the other, I was a catastrophe on two legs. This gap needed some bridging. The first step to a reasonable understanding of myself was to accept that whatever I really was had been submerged in a sea of booze for a long time. Putting a cork in the bottle had to be at the top of my list if I was ever going to achieve reasonable self-knowledge. As the haze began to burn off, I abandoned the extremes of my self-assessment for the middle ground. I was a good-hearted person with more than enough talent to make it in life who happened to be an alcoholic. A better life was about building on the former and recovering from the latter. Facing my shortcomings was a necessary starting point. Fixing what I could of my past and putting the rest into perspective came next. Paying a lot more attention to others and to the world around me shifted my focus outward. Everything got better.

Easy does it.

Bill Wilson was a wily salesman, and he takes some advertising license with this time-honored AA saying. First, the Twelve Steps are simple but not always easy. Second, the AA program is based on action—you can't work the Steps from a hammock or during commercials. I think "easy does it" is a warning to the compulsive dervish most alcoholics become at some point or another. By the time I got to rehab, I was largely unable to sleep, think straight, complete a task, conduct simple human interactions, or plan anything beyond my next trip to the liquor store. Part of what made rehab so effective for me was that I was forced out of most of that frenzy for four weeks, which gave me time to start to unwind myself for the first time in years. This saying is also a useful reminder that we alcoholics are often impulsive, anxious, angry, and confused about things. Taking a breath before speaking or acting in these situations is probably a good idea for us.

Find your bottom, save your ass.

"Bottom" refers to the place we get to in life where the need to do something about our drinking becomes undeniable. It's different for everyone, and it can range from being dead drunk and sleeping under a bridge to being asked to resign from the country club for peeing on the fairway. Early AAs were mostly chronic drunks with multiple hospital stays, seriously messed-up lives, and dim prospects. In fact, well into the 1950s, most AA chapters did not waste time on "high-bottom" drunks, since they were thought not to have suffered enough to have the motivation required to get sober. Today, drunks of all description are welcomed into AA meetings around the world. It doesn't really matter how far down you've gone, just what direction your life is headed. Each person defines his or her bottom and decides that that's far enough. At a speaker meeting one evening, a classic high-bottom drunk was telling her story of some years of heavy drinking on the LPGA tour. A thirtysomething next to me muttered, "Shit, I drank more on spring break than she drank in her whole life." We both laughed, but we knew that each person comes to AA only when they are no-kidding out of other options, and every AA respects that.

First things first.

Like many of the sayings in AA, this one has been around for a long time. And, as you might imagine, there's a particular AA slant. Many of us seem to get overwhelmed easily. I found myself sinking beneath the waves from time to time, usually because in my grandiose phases I would take on too much. Promising too much can mean delivering little or nothing. I'm told that alcoholics are accomplished procrastinators. Here, too, I was guilty. Putting first things first is another way of reminding myself to set priorities and work through them.

I always thought I did my best work under pressure. Since I was a procrastinator, that was inevitable. But setting priorities takes away the pressure, and I've found that the quality of my work has improved. Volume is up too. But if you think sobriety will remove your alcoholic quirkiness, fear not. One of the first things I now do every morning is make my bed. This symbolizes the action I will put into living my program today and the good order my program will infuse into my life. My wife appreciates the gesture, although she probably thinks it's a little peculiar.

Get sober, stay sober, live sober.

This is the progression of the AA program. Most of us came in only to get sober. An oldtimer once told me that he believed no more than 25 percent of folk at any given AA meeting were actually living the Twelve Steps—the rest were just coming to meetings to stay sober. I was a pretty good candidate for that plan. I thought that if I could get sober and stay sober, my troubles would be over and I could go back to my old, but improved, life. The AA trick in this is that I learned I could have a sober life that put my old life on its best day to shame. Also, living sober is the best insurance policy I can imagine against relapse. Living sober for me is the same thing as living undrunk.

God provides for the robin, but he doesn't deliver the worm to the nest.

This saying was probably first uttered in a Charlie Chan movie that Bill Wilson saw when he was hammered. It does have meaning for the AA though. Ours is a program of action. We refer to working the Steps, not contemplating them. Prayer of the "if you give me this, I'll do that" variety is discouraged. In my drinking days, I specialized in worry and procrastination. AA discourages these too.

I may not be much, but I'm all I think about.

This was true of me before I came into AA. It refers to the characteristic alcoholic self-centeredness. People always laugh when someone says this at a meeting, and I can only guess that it's because a lot of us see ourselves.

If God seems distant, who moved?

This saying is probably stolen like many of the rest, but it has special meaning for alcoholics. Nearly half of the original New York and Akron AAs were atheists, agnostics, or non-believers of some stripe. In fact, a whole chapter in the Big Book is directed to the spiritually skeptical; it's called "We Agnostics." As a spiritual fellowship without a creed or doctrine, AA sought only for suffering alcoholics to accept that something greater than themselves might intervene to support their recovery. Bill Wilson and his advisors anguished over how to express this in the most inclusive manner possible. The result, many believe, is the most accessible conception of a Higher Power that exists anywhere. AA asks only that the suffering alcoholic take a step toward accepting the possibility of a Higher Power that can return him or her to sanity, and that's what this saying means for us.

If you sit in a barber chair long enough, you'll get a haircut.

Some AAs are either so confident or so stupid that they return to their old drinking buddies, watering holes, and way of life, while still expecting to remain sober. It's pretty hard to do, and that's what this saying is about. I was a characteristically impulsive alcoholic, and the temptation to do something crazy is still never far from the surface. This doesn't mean I can never go into a bar or to a party, but I have to keep an eye on my motives. Teenage boys don't buy *Playboy* for the articles.

If you walk into a propeller, you're not going to worry about which blade hit you first.

A fair percentage of people in AA today seem to be addicted to both alcohol and drugs. This is especially true of prescription drugs that are legally dispensed by unwitting (or occasionally witless) doctors. AA purists think that anyone with a problem other than alcohol should be in some other fellowship, but they're a decided minority. If alcohol is a big part of your problem, you're welcome in AA. I have a friend who was addicted to both drugs and alcohol, and he swears that alcohol is more dangerous. Unlike drugs, he says, which are fairly predictable, he never knew how loaded he'd get when he started drinking. This is a life-or-death matter, and most AAs won't quibble about what poison hurts most.

In every alcoholic, there is an obsession to drink.

There is also the mirage of drinking "normally." Recognize this? For me, the obsession about drinking was at least partly biochemical. It drove my car to the liquor store whether I wanted to go there or not. The mirage of drinking just the right, moderate amount, however, was pure self-delusion and usually kicked in just before the first drink of the day. In the end, what I really sought was to be able to drink as much as I wanted to and still be considered "normal."

Keep coming back. It works if you work it.

This chant closes every AA meeting I've ever been to. The "keep coming back" part refers to the notion that the AA message will eventually be revealed with repeated exposure. The reference to "work" is all about AA's focus on taking action in the program as the gateway to everything else. Newcomers do not typically read the Big Book, go to a meeting, and get the message. We read the Big Book (and it puzzles most of us) and go to lots of meetings—only then do we start getting the message. But just saying the program works if we work it doesn't provide much useful information about how things are done. To me, it seems like more of a cheer than anything else.

Let go and let God.

This saying unnerves some AAs. It refers to recognizing that your life is not entirely in your own hands and that, after giving some enterprise or initiative the old college try, you can turn the outcome over to your Higher Power and not worry it to death. That appeals to me, but I had to come around to it. As an alcoholic, I had spent years thinking I could work or think my way into or out of anything.

There's a good joke that captures this: A successful young businessman climbs a mountain and, while standing on the summit, loses his footing and tumbles over the side. He manages to grab on to a branch and hangs on for dear life. He shouts, "Is there anyone up there?" A celestial voice answers, "This is God. Just let go." The young man keeps hanging on but notices that the tiny branch—the only thing between him and death—is cracking. He yells, "Is there anyone else up there?"

Turning things over to a Higher Power is one of the hardest undertakings in AA. It is one of the most rewarding too.

Life on life's own terms

Reality. Things as they really are, not as I wish them to be. I don't think alcoholics are the only people in the world who filter reality to suit themselves, but we're especially good at it. Every time something unpleasant about my life presented itself, I drank it into its "proper perspective." I have yet to meet an AA who did not do this all the time. Of course, it raises hell with our lives. Getting a grip on reality is not an overnight project. For me, it's gone something like this: stop drinking, start being honest about myself and my circumstances, actually pay attention to what others say and do, trade passive for active, and fear not.

The longer I am in AA, the less tolerant I am of unreality. There is a reason for this change in me. I like reality a lot better now, and being aware of people, places, and things as they really are turns out to be the best way to manage my days. What about the tough times? Here, too, knowing the real score and acting on that basis gives me power and serenity that vodka never did for more than a flash. I'm pretty sure that trying to be a realist without being an optimist at heart would be tough. Since I got sober, I'm all about optimism, and so is AA (see also "Serenity Prayer" on page 134).

Live and let live.

Who could possibly disagree with this old saw? An alcoholic, that's who. I spent a huge amount of time during my drinking career critically assessing other people and figuring what it would take to put them right. This included everyone in my family, all my friends, everyone who worked with me, and people ahead of me in line at the movies. Occasionally, I would sense that someone else was taking my measure in the same way, which I really resented. Both of these parlor games are especially bad for alcoholics. I wasted time and energy trying to fix people I had no business even measuring for a new personality. At the same time, I was getting angry at the thought that anyone in the world would be finding fault with me. This added up to a major distraction that produced no positive result and prevented me from seeing the good in others or the flaws in myself. AAs are always talking about "cleaning up your own side of the street." That is good advice for most of us.

Live in the moment.

Wait a minute! Isn't that what I was doing when I was drinking? Not quite. This AA standby means something different from the chronic irresponsibility and selfishness of our drinking lives. As I went through the Steps, I became able to put my past in its place and recognized that there was nothing I could do to change it. I also began to appreciate how entirely unknowable tomorrow really is. That doesn't mean that we shouldn't make appropriate amends for past deeds or sensible plans for the future—AA encourages both. But our abiding reality is that we have only this moment. It is in the present that I choose all the actions that make up my past and my future. Since I sobered up, I ruminate and plot much less and live a lot more.

The mind is a dangerous place. Don't go there alone.

Self-centeredness, resentment, and self-pity are prime threats to recovering alcoholics. This saying is, in part, a reminder not to wallow in that kind of thinking. Also, most of us got in trouble trying to sort out our messed-up lives by ourselves. While introspection and self-knowledge are generally useful, self-absorption is a slippery slope for the alcoholic.

More will be revealed.

This quote is the punch line of many AA jokes, usually delivered with a knowing smile. It has a serious side, of course. It contains part of the answer to the question "What keeps people interested in and committed to AA over the long term?" There is real depth and meaning to the AA philosophy, which come to light gradually as we live the program. I was amazed by how much the Twelve Steps changed as I worked them and reflected on them over time. It's like finding a new grip with an old golf club, except now my life depends on hitting the ball straight.

No one ever got sober confessing the other guy's sins.

This was great advice, especially as I worked on Steps 4, 5, and 6 (removing my character defects) and Steps 8 and 9 (making amends to those I had harmed). Even in my most honest and candid moments, I was occasionally tempted to explain away my own bad behavior as resulting from the unreasonable, uncharitable, or unspeakable act of someone else. That usually turned out to be a self-serving reading of the episode. Where others did play a negative role, that fact was almost always irrelevant to my recovery in the long run.

> ### No tragedy or misfortune in life is so bad that a few drinks won't make it worse.

Almost every AA meeting includes a story or two about getting through one of life's rough patches without drinking. Some of the things that happen to our fellow AAs would test the strongest person. But for us, drinking will always make it worse. It is fundamental to our survival to know that people do get through tragedy without alcohol, and that doing so makes us stronger.

One day at a time

This is the best known of all the AA sayings, because it's associated with our unique recovery horizon of twenty-four hours. It's true that relief from the obsession to drink is a twenty-four-hour reprieve. Many of us go to bed at night thanking our Higher Power for a sober day and rise in the morning asking for another. But the AA concept of time goes beyond just this one-day chunk of recovery. Living sober is about noticing and feeling the moment—"living in the moment," as it's called. There's an old saw about life being what happens while you're making your plans. AA's approach is very similar. We work toward the future we want and think is right for us, but not at the expense of living in the present too. When I started to get sober, I was very skeptical about buying into another master plan because I'd been disappointed by many unfulfilled wishes and dreams over the years. Many AAs are like this. But when we start doing all the "right" things we can every day, life does get better. Maybe we don't get exactly what we want, but as the philosopher Mick Jagger said, we get what we need. I don't pretend to know how this works, but I've seen it over and over in my own life and among AA friends.

Poor me, poor me, pour me another drink.

When self-centered people like me don't get our way, we shift into self-pity faster than Dale Earnhardt Jr. in the passing lane. Booze was my reliable companion and infallible tonic when the world failed to understand my talents or needs. I heard something about this in a meeting that got my attention: "We can't feel resentment or self-pity when we're not thinking about ourselves." Putting my mental energies toward helping another alcoholic, for example, is one surefire way to beat self-pity and the drinking that often accompanied it in my life.

Stick with the winners.

This saying is meant to encourage newcomers to watch, imitate, and hang with people who are clearly doing well in the program. I had no trouble with this. I wanted to have what these winners obviously had as soon as I could get my hands on it. The downside is that if the focus is exclusively on success, some struggling AAs might not get the support they need at crucial junctures. But that doesn't actually happen in practice, because the winners understand better than anyone that they must share their experience, strength, and hope widely if they expect to keep it. I think this is another example of AA's many self-correcting and self-regulating mechanisms at work.

There are no coincidences in God's world.

I don't entirely believe this old AA saw. I think it implies a degree of predetermination that would take some of the challenge and fun out of even sober life. Much in life is out of our hands, and unless you believe we're just spinning aimlessly in space, all that must be controlled somewhere. That much I can accept. But expecting that my Higher Power knows where I'm going to dinner tonight and who I'll run into seems like a slippery slope toward zero responsibility. (That might be very attractive to a lot of alcoholics.) Step 3 says we turn our will over to the *care* of a Higher Power, not that we forfeit it. I do buy that many things in life we view as incidental probably happen for a reason that is beyond us at the moment. As my mother told me years ago, even bad things can lead to positive ends. I'm sure I'll get some negative feedback for this definition, but being an alcoholic, I'm sure I'm right.

There is a God, and it's not me.

I always saw myself as a rugged individualist. Actually I was a prima donna and fairly lonely. Alcoholics are subject to "self-will run riot," according to page 62 of the Big Book, and I certainly was. Accepting a "Power greater than ourselves" is the heart of Step 2 and opens the way for a lot of good things in AA (see "Spirituality" on page 36). This is not about religion, by the way. It's more about recognizing that self-centeredness is wrecking our lives and we really need to find another North Star. This is important, and I found that listening in meetings whenever self-will came up was a good thing for me.

Think before you drink, and call before you fall.

This saying is a good candidate for a highway patrol billboard. It's designed to remind AAs of two deadly weaknesses that many of us share: impulsiveness and a tendency to go it alone. If we really thought about the drink we are considering and recalled where drinking led us last time, we would probably not hoist away. Also, if the fever is really on us, a call to our sponsor or another AA will almost always extinguish the blaze.

Think, think, think.

You'll see this on the wall of most AA meeting rooms. It comes from the original AA concept and emphasizes the mental component of both our disease and our recovery. People who merely stop drinking (see "dry drunk" on page 109) generally do not address the warped way of thinking that characterizes alcoholism, so they never get fully sober. In my old life, I was able to talk myself into almost anything if it included a drink. I rarely thought about the consequences; if I did, I just vowed that things would be different this time. Thinking can become a key ally in sobriety if we let it. For example, focusing on gratitude in moments of mental stress is a terrific gimmick to remind ourselves of all the good things we can lose if we drink. The point is simply that alcoholism has a mental component, and we need to be on guard against our own mind's capacity to take us for a terrible ride if we let it. (For the opposite of this, see "stinkin' thinkin'" on page 137.)

We aren't a glum lot.

This comes from page 132 of the Big Book, and I've heard it a hundred times. What can I say? AA meetings—with their famous drunkalogs (see page 108) and outrageous sharing episodes—can be very funny. In fact, I've never been to a meeting that didn't have some funny parts, and some meetings have been downright hilarious. How can this life-or-death subject be treated lightly? First, I think there's an honored role for laughter in recovery from any affliction. Second, it beats crying (of which there's plenty in AA). Third, escapades while drinking can be truly funny, and AA meetings are the only setting in which most of us would ever mention some of this stuff. Trying to learn how to live a sober life can be equally funny. Going to an AA meeting is not like going to a comedy club, but I've always found a healthy lightness of heart and acceptance of life as it really is.

You have to give it away to keep it.

Bill and Bob had been battling their alcoholism for years without getting sober until they started sharing their experiences with each other and other drunks. This was the soul of AA for the founders, and it's the message in Step 12. Sponsorship is about sharing the message, and so is the AA meeting. All forms of AA service are part of sharing experience, strength, and hope with the still-suffering alcoholic. Far from evangelism, this is a quiet bond between the recovering and active drunk that heals both. I'm not sure how this works, but there's a lot of psychic mojo flowing when these encounters take place.

CHAPTER 7

One-Year Progress Report

I've made a number of claims in these pages regarding the effectiveness of the AA program among the fellowship's 2 million members. Since our membership is anonymous, we're not in a position to do comprehensive studies on ourselves in order to bear out these claims. But before I ask you to take it all on faith, I can offer a case study of one: myself. Admittedly, the sample size is small, but my confidence in the data is high. Since alcoholism is a disease of body, mind, and spirit, let me commence along those lines.

Body

Most of us in AA stopped drinking for various periods before we got serious about quitting for good. I certainly did. Usually under family pressure, I would quit for a month or so. I once quit for three months. Since I never really intended that this would be permanent, I didn't get panicky about not having booze around. After about a week of fairly mild discomfort, I was usually okay. I probably quit like this eight or ten times over the years.

It amazed me how good I felt when I didn't drink and how fast I started feeling good. I slept better and my energy level went way up. I was less anxious and more fun. But in my alcoholic mind, I twisted these signals from my body to mean that I could quit successfully anytime I wanted to, and sooner or later, the good feelings became something to celebrate with a drink.

By the time I hit bottom, I could no longer stop at will, and this scared me. When I was admitted to detox, my blood alcohol content was three times the legal limit, and getting my blood pressure down to a noncritical level that first night was difficult. Detox and the first few days of rehab were a bitch. Even with Librium and some other stuff, I was shaking like a leaf, alternating between hot flashes and chills, unable to eat anything, and severely disoriented. My mood swung from irritated to furious, and I would have done nearly anything for a pint of vodka. When my blood tests came back a few days after I entered rehab, the doctor told me how very sick I was. I was scared.

Today I can honestly say that I've never been in better physical shape as an adult. My blood chemistry is normal and so is my blood pressure. Liver function is normal, and I miraculously suffered no permanent damage there. I sleep like a champ and eat in a healthy way. I've lost a considerable amount of weight, and since I go to the local gym several days a week, I'm in good shape. The puffiness in my face has disappeared, and my skin color and tone have returned to normal. People comment on the sparkle in my eyes often enough for me to believe that something good is happening there too. My normal balance has returned, the ringing in my ears has gone away, and I no longer snore. The racing heart, panicky elevated respiration, and breathlessness from minor exertion are gone. I feel calm, even under pressure, and I have more energy than I know what to do with. Best of all, I have absolutely no physical craving for alcohol. None.

Mind

I'm pretty sure I was certifiably nuts by the end of my last drinking binge. Half of me was an oblivious drunk, while the other half was a paranoid person given to inappropriate remarks and unable to hold a coherent thought for more than a couple minutes. I had no judgment, and reality for me was always open to discussion. On my last morning in the office, I couldn't sign the paychecks because my hand was shaking so much. I made a mental note to return to that task after I had gotten my morning ration of grog. By the time I got around to the checks again, I couldn't sign them because I was too drunk. When I was released from detox after nearly having a coronary, I immediately banged back a few drinks. When my wife told me the next day that we were going to rehab, I responded with a straight face that I was "not ready." My head was seriously messed up.

Mentally I'm now sharper than I have been in years. My thinking is logical and unhurried. My memory is as good as it ever was. I'm intellectually curious again and have almost entirely abandoned TV for reading. My creative juices are flowing, and my sense of humor is sharp. I'm able to plan and organize as I could many years ago. This means that everything from work and projects to bills and calendar are in order. By the end of my drinking days, I couldn't plan anything beyond a day or two out. Now I enjoy scheduling events and travel months in advance. I'm handling money with ease, and it seems to be going farther. My days are orderly and I'm amazed at how much I can fit into twenty-four hours. I make time for friends and family every day. Keeping things in perspective has become natural, and I'm rarely exasperated or impatient. I'm mostly interested, charmed, or amused by things around me in the world. I smell roses when I pass them.

Spirit

It was easy to make major progress in my spiritual life after I quit drinking, because while I was drinking I had no spiritual life. Aside from the odd foxhole prayer over the years, I had little use for God. Today, I rarely begin a day without prayer and meditation. When I don't make time to address my Higher Power in the morning, I invariably find that the wheels come off the day sooner or later. In everything I do, I try to remain aware of how I might be affecting others. I try to be positive, tolerant, and cheerful. I rarely harm another person; if I do, I try to put the situation right as quickly as I can. If this sounds impossibly complicated and goody-goody, try it for a month or two. Being civil to others is not that hard, and I was surprised at the terrific reaction from people I work with or meet in the course of a day. People respond to simple courtesies and basic human kindness. All this makes *me* feel very good too. Remember, each AA defines Higher Power as he or she chooses. The power of the spiritual concept lies not in the definition itself, but in our acceptance that there is something out there that is bigger than we are. Considering the dog's breakfast my life had become by the time I got to AA, I was ready to believe this.

Four Key Areas

I've lost track of how much in my life has improved since I came into AA. I believe the Spanish word for it is *mucho*. But a few key areas bear special mention, because many alcoholics seem to have trouble with the same stuff and often see the biggest changes here. I'm referring to fear, resentment, anger, and defects of character.

Fear

By the time I'd finished with Step 4, I had identified no fewer than nine different fears that were regularly haunting me. No wonder I drank! In priority order, they were fear of authority, failure, being found out as a fraud, abandonment, trust, my impulsiveness, my urge to please others, pity, and danger. When I really looked at myself, I was stunned at how much damage these fears had wrought in my life and in the lives of those around me. I started right away asking my Higher Power to remove my fears, and in very short order, they began to fade. Today, some are gone altogether and others are pale imitations of the goblins they once were.

That's not to say that some things don't still scare me for no good reason. Psychologists call it "the rope in the road": things that are not what we think they are, like the snake in the road that's really a rope but scares us just the same. For instance, I can still put off a phone call or a meeting because I think the outcome will not be good. I did a lot of that in my drinking days. But now, if something frightens me, I'm at least more likely to confront it than not. Don't confuse this with fearlessness—I'm not fearless. But I do feel as though most of my life unfolds within a kind of safety zone. If I'm doing the right things for the right reasons, nothing weird is likely to come down. It still takes a little discipline to act despite feelings of fear, but it no longer takes a drink.

Resentment

I'm willing to bet that no other demographic produces more righteous indignation than alcoholics. If there was a market for it, we could pay off the national debt. Even at my most successful, I felt that others were enjoying accolades and rewards meant for me. As I drank more and my troubles mounted, my resentment grew. Even if the mess was my fault, it was easy for me to believe that someone else was to blame. This is part of what it means to be "blind drunk."

After I'd been in AA for a while, it became clear to me that figuring out who's to blame is irrelevant in most cases. Resentment, justified or imagined, was eating me up either way. But the remedy flogged in AA is counterintuitive for most of us alcoholics. "Just let it go" was the blithe counsel I kept getting. But my brain had always told me that a beef will nag you unless you settle the score. What can I say? This is not only wrong but stupid. Score-settling is a low-percentage game that we almost never win. When I was drinking, I got into a business deal with a big, tough Boston Irishman. We were screwed in the deal, and I was sure my partner would be calling out some of his Guinness-soaked hooligan friends. To my surprise, his only comment about the guys who gamed us was "Don't even ignore the bastards." I carried that puzzling comment around for a long time, never understanding what he meant until I got to AA.

Resentments are tricky though. After months of believing that I had my big ones all but banished, I developed a huge resentment toward a close friend more or less out of the blue. That was painful for us both and some damage was done. But most of the time, I truly believe that resentments are dead weight, and I try to carry around as few as possible.

Anger

Anger is another commodity I wish I could monetize—I'd be rich. My anger spectrum as a drinker went from chronic impatience to touchiness to rants. I was never violent, and I never hurt anyone or broke anything. I saved my fiercest anger for solitary moments when I could drink up appropriate solutions to my problem of the day. I was way beyond making a list of pros and cons or taking a long walk to deal with anger. I just got mad and got drunk.

They told me in rehab that anger is a manifestation of fear. That only made me angrier because I just *knew* anger was caused by other people screwing me. Of course, as I settled down and started to open my mind to alternative explanations, I recognized the relationship between fear and anger. Being afraid made me anxious. Anxiety made me feel vulnerable. Vulnerability signaled loss of control. Feeling out of control made me angry. Anger masked my fear for a while. Bingo! The problem with this loop was that it never identified or addressed what I was afraid of to begin with. I could always count on more trouble from the same source.

I still get peeved from time to time, but I usually recognize what's happening and try to deal with it. Certain things—like getting cut off in traffic—are easy to fix. Forget about it and drive. Other causes of anger might take some figuring out. For example, as a recovering alcoholic, I'm occasionally patronized by people from my former life who feel sorry for me. Since I can't give a long speech about how much better off I am now, I have to endure the pity. That would make me angry if it weren't for my new confidence in two things. First, the other person most likely means me no harm and is responding to me in the most charitable fashion at hand. Second, what I really don't like about the situation is that I can't boast about my accomplishments in recovery. That's self-centeredness—a separate problem entirely.

Staying even-tempered with those closest to me has, for some reason, proved to be the hardest. I have the best intentions, but my shiny new AA tools sometimes fail me with this vital constituency. When I do get my knickers in a twist and there's collateral damage to another person, I try to set things right as soon as I realize what's going on. That is sometimes not enough, but in my experience, others are often pleasantly surprised and very responsive when I move quickly to make things right.

Defects of Character

Alcoholics are not alone in this world in having defective characters. The difference for us is that our defects can kill us, so working on removing them becomes uniquely urgent. During my first few months in AA, I compiled quite a list of shortcomings. In fact, my list was so extensive that I became a little pessimistic about ever whittling it down. Fortunately for me, my sponsor and some other veteran AAs let me in on a secret: Pick the defects you think you can make some progress on and work on those first. If you make some headway, that's great. If not, switch to different ones. One of the things I really like about AA is that there's no shame in picking low-hanging fruit.

Here are the character flaws I've chosen to work on so far. Others await attention. I'm not a slacker, and in the world of AA, my list is respectably ambitious.

Pride

I think the adage "pride cometh before a fall" is from the Bible. Wherever it comes from, the saying really nails it for me. Even when I was at my worst and most pathetic, I was almost always proud of myself for something. Maybe it was my position or my charm, my material possessions or my experiences, my education, my wife, or my precocious children. Anyone could tell I was a player. Sometimes I felt the need to do something nice for others—lucky them! Today, I try to turn my feelings of self-worship into humility. It can be hard. I am not a sackcloth-and-ashes kind of person, but most of us have plenty to be humble about. For the record, humility feels good and seems to breed strength.

Superiority Complex

This is the handmaiden of pride. I was convinced even at my bottom that I was a uniquely gifted individual. My intellect and talents would dazzle you if only you'd pay attention. I took this attitude with me to my early AA meetings and into rehab. Between being called out by other equally "gifted" drunks and beginning to see myself and the world as they really are, I've gotten some perspective. But I'm not cured. A few months ago, I suffered a crisis of confidence about my AA program. I noticed that people seemed to like what I was saying in meetings and found that I was enjoying the attention. Then, all of a sudden, I became convinced that everything I said was crap. Just like that. For a while, I couldn't bring myself to share at all. I started switching groups every week or so to see if I could shake it off. It's still not fixed, but things are getting better. I'm more careful about what I say in meetings, and the old confidence is gone for the time being. On balance, though, I still think I do a lot of things pretty well, but now I tend to think of setting and meeting personal goals as job one for me. I'll leave the pursuit of genius and celebrity to people who actually have a chance at it.

Procrastination

I have yet to meet an alcoholic who didn't chronically defer important things. I got late notices when I had the money in the bank to pay the bills. I paid full airline fares even when I knew a trip was coming up months before. I let my lawnmower run out of oil. I never mailed a change of address card before I'd been in the new place at least three months. The antidote for procrastination has nothing directly to do with AA. We all learn it in Sunday School or some similar venue. It's industry. But because I was an active alcoholic, my procrastination was oddly fear-driven. I regularly put things off because I was somehow frightened about tackling them. That's hard to fathom, since the consequences of not acting were invariably worse. Procrastination has proven hard to beat entirely.

Envy

Have you ever noticed how many people confuse envy and jealousy? Jealousy is about people and envy is about things. As a drinker, I was supremely materialistic and I felt a fair amount of envy of others no matter how much I had. Now that I'm sober, I still like nice things. The difference is that I have a clearer idea about what I actually need in life and what I simply want. This is a great relief, because the Joneses always seem to outspend me. In place of envy, I try to give some regular thought to gratitude, and I have so much to be grateful for that it's almost embarrassing to want more.

Lust

From what I've heard around AA meetings, unchained lust is a common affliction among alcoholics. As a group, we are victims of arrested development, according to many psychiatrists. While we were drinking, our judgment reliably shorted out. This perfect storm of immaturity made for some bad scenes for most of us. In addition to being ashamed and mortified by my weakness, I've concluded that lust is oversold. Love is vastly superior, and lust is included in the love concept anyway. So I'm opting for love.

Self-Centeredness

No one thinks about himself or herself more than an alcoholic, except perhaps a politician (and I suspect that many politicians are alcoholics). The alcoholic brain somehow zeros in on itself, and we soon begin to destroy ourselves through narcissism. In the later stages of my drinking, I became reclusive. If all one thinks about is oneself, why have company? Reconnecting with other people and life is essential to recovery, but it's not always easy. I hadn't really made friends or shared interests with others or "put myself out there" in any way for a long time while I was drinking. I couldn't just wake up one morning and join Toastmasters.

One good answer to isolation for us lies in service. Service for AAs is getting into good enough physical, mental, and spiritual shape to be able to help another alcoholic or to help others when the opportunity arises. From a kind word to a national project, it's all service. It's not possible to be selfish when we're doing things for others. Since drowning in ourselves means death for alcoholics, most of us are kindly disposed to service.

Sport Criticism

I made this term up to describe the habitual taking of another person's measure from a fixed, critical viewpoint. In AA, I was told that alcoholics are bigger offenders on this count than the general population. Maybe, but I've known some nonalcoholics who also love nothing more than taking people apart for the fun of it. The special peril in this for alcoholics is that we can't afford the blinding effect of this game on our own shortcomings, which are busy wrecking our lives and killing us. What a relief it was to find that when I started to substitute tolerance for criticism, I didn't miss the fun of taking the other person's inventory as much as I thought I would. I still do this now and then, but I'm not as nasty about it, I immediately feel guilty, and I recognize that people are sizing me up for a laugh too.

I've offered this summary to illustrate how I worked the AA program and how the AA program worked for me during my first twelve months in the fellowship. It has been wonderful, although not trouble free. Just because this is how it played out for me doesn't necessarily mean the storyline will be the same for the next person. But a lot of what happened to me—and for me—over the past year was also happening all around me for other AAs.

The absolute best news I ever got in my life came with AA: I had a second chance. Everyone in AA gets one of life's very rare second bites at the apple. Of course, you don't have to be an alcoholic to reinvent yourself, but falling apart is a real incentive to rebuilding. Unlike my "normal" friends, I was an alcoholic in crisis, and I knew that nothing short of a top-to-bottom transformation of my life could fix what was broken inside me. Seeing and feeling this transformation unfold has been the biggest surprise of my life and as close to a miracle as I may ever get.

At one year sober, I'm not yet ready to say that I'm grateful for being an alcoholic. There are aspects of being an alcoholic that are very painful. But I honestly can't imagine what other path I might have taken to where I am today. Speaking of today, I also understand with crystal clarity that my recovery is for today only. I renew my acceptance of alcoholism in my life and my commitment to AA every day. I am comfortable—free, really—in my sobriety, but relapse is part of this disease and no one is immune. I think it's a fact of life that a certain amount of danger and potential tragedy lurk in the shadows for all of us. But I know where one of my biggest goblins is hiding, and I keep vigilant watch.

CHAPTER 8

Other People

AA would be little more than a stop-drinking gimmick if it weren't for the profound, durable effect it has on the personal lives of its members. We become able to change. Here is what I mean.

My personal life occurs at the point of contact between me and the world around me, and a number of factors are at work in the collision. My physical self interacts with the physical world, and I see the mountains, hear the rustle of the breeze, and feel my wife's hand in mine. I can also occasionally connect with what I believe is a spiritual universe around me. Things I used to dismiss as only a hunch, a feeling, intuition, or sometimes just a coincidence, I am now inclined to take more seriously. So, when I think about changing things in my life, I have some choices. I can try to change the physical world, but that is not always easy. Or I can try to change the subconscious universe around me, but that sounds too hard. Or I can choose to change myself. Once I really thought about it, working on me seemed like the easiest approach. It is also the AA approach.

Most of us would probably agree that the expression "What have you done for me today?" is arrogant and uncharitable. It captures much of what I was as a drinker. I don't think about other people in this selfish way any more, but I confess that I often examine the results of my AA work. I love my new way of life precisely because I receive positive, tangible returns on my personal investment every day. I see an unmistakable correlation between doing the right thing and having right things happen in my life. I don't know how this works, but I have no doubt that it does. And nowhere has this been more dramatic than in my relationships with other people.

The train wreck we alcoholics make of our relationships is a hallmark of our affliction. Drinking makes us shallow, selfish, and unreliable. Others see this long before we do and eventually avoid us or drop us. By the end of my drinking career, the good-hearted, outgoing A.J. had become a lonely, bitter person. In those rare moments of self-examination after the first couple drinks of the day, I occasionally thought about what it would take to reclaim even a small part of my former health and happiness. This depressed me no end and always required more vodka to lift my spirits. I was misunderstood, mistreated, and very underappreciated. And I was absolutely convinced that the fault lay with others.

Of course, that was not true at all. Other people were not my problem, but they did turn out to be my solution. Once I admitted to another drunk that I was a drunk too, I embarked on the biggest building project of my life. With only a seventy-year-old book as a blueprint, I began to construct a network of friends and acquaintances that today are the source of much of my courage, strength, and hope. Unlike previous attempts at networking, I traded scheming for listening and taking an interest in others.

Marriage

But what about the relationships that mean the most? Good question. Let's talk about those. The relationship that AAs seem especially adept at destroying is marriage. I was in a car early in my sobriety with three veteran AAs on the way to a meeting. The subject of matrimony came up, and it turned out that we had eleven marriages among us (I only had one). Not all AAs can boast three or four trips to the altar, but there does seem to be a *Groundhog Day* quality to marriage for many alcoholics.

Alcoholism is so nasty that many marriages simply don't survive it. That's almost a certainty if the afflicted partner doesn't sober up. Marriages that are rescued by AA or something else may not be bulletproof, but I believe that those marriages have a better than even chance against anything else life might throw at them. A short twelve months ago, I saw years of marriage to a fabulous person about to go over the falls. I was panicked but without a plan (or the courage to make one) that included giving up drinking for good. Today, my marriage is stronger and happier than it ever has been.

This is no exaggeration, and I've seen the same thing happen with other AAs. Why and how such a desperate situation turned around the way it did is still part miracle and part mystery for me. I do, however, know how to keep my marriage healthy—stay sober and live my program. Before I oversell this, let me state the obvious: not every marriage can or should be rescued. Of the ones that can, each transformation will unfold in its own way. Here's how things played out for me.

A lot of people talk about alcoholics in terms of a Dr. Jekyll and Mr. Hyde personality split that baffles everyone, including the drunk. As my drinking got worse, I was increasingly two different people. The sober A.J. was cheerful, industrious, and kind. The drunk A.J. was moody, grandiose, and selfish. I was aware of the personality flip-flop and tried to stay in the Good A.J. personality as long as I could whenever I drank. My wife gave me effort points for this and for my sincere-sounding promises to control my drinking. But two things happened that put my marriage on a dangerous footing and forced everyone's hand.

First, my ability to shift from Jekyll to Hyde and back again began to disappear. Even sober, I was increasingly negative, paranoid, and cranky. Second, my wife's patience and hope turned increasingly to despair and anger. The marriage was off the rails, and we both knew it. Alcoholism was the culprit. We were both terribly sad, but only action on my part could change things.

Accepting my alcoholism and getting to rehab and AA saved my life and my marriage. Doing those things finally seemed possible for two reasons: (1) I had run out of other options and (2) my wife was willing to support me. Her support was a huge source of courage and hope. Since no subject was off-limits in rehab, I heard a lot about other people's struggles with marriage and getting sober. A few were as lucky as I was and had a spouse who was really in their corner. Others had spouses who were alcoholics too, and they didn't have much of a chance if the other person was still drinking. Some people discovered, to their surprise, that the anticipated joy and respect for their efforts was not forthcoming because their spouse was invested in the relationship in its unhealthy form and felt deeply threatened by their determination to get well. Others came out of rehab ready to move on, only to find a partner whose relief at their sobriety had given way to a hurricane of resentment over past troubles. A few found "better" partners in rehab and were clearly gearing up for a new round of trouble.

Between my wife and me, there was some circling of one another after I got home from rehab. I desperately wanted to project my new confidence and commitment, and she just as desperately wanted to believe me. But years of bad behavior and broken promises had to be overcome, and like a lot of things in life, a process was involved. The first part of our relationship that came back was conversation. Toward the end of my drinking, I'd become so touchy about the subject of alcohol that I avoided conversation in general. We'd always had some of our best conversations on long hikes. I had increasingly found excuses to avoid these outings, fearing that I'd be stranded out in the boondocks with nothing but the truth for company.

Conversation led to a reawakening of the humor we both love. We're two funny characters, and after rehab, we had some terrific new material. AA provided plenty of laughs too. Humor took the sting out of the past and seemed to relax us in the moment. A well-aimed quip could soften a bad memory and move the conversation toward more hopeful themes. Naturally, not everything was hilarious, but I was surprised at how much was. Being able to talk and laugh together opened the way to the serious business of rebuilding our mutual trust and our confidence in the future. If you're lucky, everything leads to intimacy. I don't mean just sex, but full-spectrum intimacy. In my opinion, that's the cornerstone of any successful marriage and life's brass ring. As I said, getting from where I was to where I am is part miracle and part mystery. None of it would have happened without AA.

Once I got started, I became a little frantic about keeping the post-booze relationship with my wife strong. My instinct was to keep doing what I was doing and hope for continued good results. But it would take more than that. Because my wife had borne much of my affliction at close quarters and sacrificed some of her life to see me through it, I would forever owe her a special debt of gratitude. It's not about flowers every Tuesday or a daily stream of compliments. This account can only be settled on my last day and only if I've been the best companion I can be on every intervening day. This is called a "living amend," and I undertake it each day, not from obligation or remorse but with gratitude that I was given a second chance to get things right.

Children

There's nothing more painful to contemplate for most alcoholics than the damage we did to our children during our drinking days. I'm haunted by this. I never fell into corporal punishment, but I knew how to scare and humiliate my children in the name of "discipline." I remember one day on a family vacation when my wife and I were playing doubles tennis with our kids. Our older son missed a shot and threw a little fit. I showed him a thing or two about fits, loudly calling him a jerk and threatening all manner of mayhem if he didn't start to have fun immediately. I can still remember the shock among the players on the adjoining courts and my wife's mortification. Most of all, I remember the frightened look on my son's face. I was hungover and I was a bully. Nice memory for both of us. There were more of them like that over the years.

Unlike our spouses, who choose to cast their lot with us, our children are along for the ride whether they want to be or not. Also, as an adult, my wife could let me know when I was getting toward the edge of crazy and draw a line in the sand. So I had a better chance of avoiding hurtful stupidity with her, even if I chose to go ahead anyway. Bullying the children was only half the story. As they got older, I developed a knack for embarrassing them when I was drunk. This was not just about thinking a "mullet" was a fish or that "groovy" was still a pop-culture word. More often it was just me being drunk and the kids knowing it. My outbursts might intimidate them, but my boozy, jolly self scared them, and I think that may have been worse.

The good news about my children is really good. They always wanted to believe the best about me, and they apparently still do. There's something hardwired into humans that permits us to insist that "my dad can beat up your dad" or "my mom was Miss America." The remedy for me as an alcoholic parent was not complicated: stop drinking and start being a better person. I was lucky because the damage was not horrendous. Also, my kids are older, so I've been able to speak frankly with them about my alcoholism. I can tell it's a lot for them to digest, but they want to understand and they're thrilled that I'm doing so much better, no matter why that is.

I come from a line of alcoholics, and I pray it stops with

me, so I don't pull any punches with my children about alcohol. Of course, there's no substitute for showing them that I've found a much better way to live. Children can be skeptical, and they want to know how you get the good things in life. I have to be living proof that my own life is happy and full, and offer a glimpse of what the good things really are.

Family

Families come in all sizes and varieties. I love my family. We moved around a lot while I was growing up, and I think that made us closer. Some of my siblings, cousins, aunts, and uncles are alcoholics. Some are not. While I was still drinking, no one in my family called me on it, partly because drinking was such a part of our family culture and partly because we all lived in different places, so we didn't see each other on a regular basis. Also, we're Welsh/English and thus tend to be a reserved and discreet bunch. For example, we never discussed sex or money because those were private matters. Drinking fit nicely into the off-limits category.

When I went to rehab and started to get sober, the family reaction generally followed drinker/nondrinker lines. My sober relatives (especially the ones who are familiar with AA) were delighted for me. Others said little or nothing. I was too busy figuring things out for myself to pay much attention to the reactions. Today, I appreciate the support of those who offered it, and I'm not at all sore about the silence from others. Alcoholism has become more accepted as part of our social scene, but people are rarely neutral on the subject. I'm willing to talk about it if someone else wants to and am just as willing to shut up if it makes the other person uncomfortable. My job is to stay sober.

Friends

I was a lot more worried than I should have been about what my friends were going to think of me after I got out of rehab. I was prepared for the worst, although when I first got home, I was totally focused on recovery and didn't give much thought to these relationships. That's not to say that I didn't have a desire to be accepted again by those who knew me as a drinker. Or that I didn't want to be recognized as a survivor and a winner. But the reality of those early days for me was the absolute necessity of getting my close relationships rebalanced and figuring out how to make it in AA.

When I turned outward again, I found that former friends reacted in some pretty standard ways. Most of them were thrilled for me. In fact, one of the biggest surprises of my return to real life was how many people had known I was a mess and how many of them found joy in my recovery. Some people, though, were cool to the new me. The most obviously uncomfortable were former drinking companions. Some of those folks have seen fit to move on—maybe they thought I'd try to evangelize them, or maybe drinking was all we ever had in common. That's okay with me. I hope they can drink without becoming drunks; if they can't, I hope they latch on to AA before it's too late. A few former friends seemed intimidated by my new way of living, maybe because they were more comfortable looking down on me or maybe because they sense that alcoholism is zeroing in on them. Others lamented that they liked the "old A.J." better. They're mostly alcoholics themselves, and I hope they get to AA.

Colleagues

Then there are my former colleagues and associates. Most of them were not actually friends, but I spent a lot of time with them. They knew more about me than I would have guessed. The arrogance that came with my drinking caused me to largely ignore my colleagues, as I didn't consider most of them terribly important to my happiness or success. Not surprisingly, they noticed that and were not pleased. The colleague and associate pool was the source of some particularly nasty gossip and hard feelings, most of which I probably deserved.

I am no longer working at the same place, so I haven't been in a position to set much of this mess right, although I have where I could. The best thing I can do is to live my life well and trust that this will constitute a kind of redress for past sins. I don't resent former colleagues who dumped me, and I appreciate those who gave me the benefit of the doubt when I went into rehab. I sometimes feel as though I was radioactive to former business associates for longer than I deserved after I got sober, but that's beyond my control. I know that the best way to demonstrate my readiness for a professional comeback is to actually have my professional act together. This seems to be working: the same grapevine that consigned me to the junk heap a year ago is resurrecting me today.

Occasionally I see a former colleague, and these encounters have not been all bad. I'm not the puffy, red-faced, grandiose person they once knew, and that seems to have a good effect. Bottom line, though, is that most people have not given me much thought.

That brings up one of the biggest—and ultimately funniest—surprises to me in sobriety: *many people, even in my own family, don't know or care that I was an alcoholic and I sobered up.* People don't notice or care that I don't drink at parties. People don't notice or care that I have a wonderful new life. During my drinking years, I assumed—the way teenagers do—that everyone who passed through my life noticed everything about me and cared about it. I admit that it's been something of a shock to discover that my life is primarily of interest only to me, and that other people—even the people who love me—are mainly interested in (guess what?) *their own lives.*

Strangers

I was never very friendly to strangers unless I was hammered—after all, they were strangers. I felt superior to many people and had a very uncharming way of ignoring or patronizing them. Never much of a smiler, I seemed to frighten people I met casually, and in fact, I took some pleasure in that. This has all changed during the past year.

I'm now a fairly friendly person, and I smile at strangers all the time. I talk to people in stores or at the gas station or at the gym. I'm civil to telemarketers and never give anyone the finger in traffic. No one is more surprised than I am about this transformation. Like much of my new behavior, there's a reinforcing loop at work here. First, other people respond well when I'm friendly and that makes me want to be friendly again. Smiles beget smiles. Even the briefest interaction with a total stranger can be fun, and that, in turn, can become a habit.

Every once in a while, a greeting turns into a conversation of surprising depth. Here's an example. I'd been saying hi to Augie at the gym for a few months. He's the guy who maintains the equipment and generally fixes stuff around the place. One day he mentioned that working on cardio equipment was a lot easier than the heavy farm equipment he spent most of his life maintaining. Before I knew it, I was getting interested in his story about wheat farming on the Great Plains.

I learned that Augie had reluctantly moved back to the farm from his city job in the early 1970s to support his parents and ended up staying there for twenty-five years. He shared the story of his parents' economic collapse during the Depression and his own self-doubt about his farming moxie. I told him that I'd learned all I knew about farming in the Safeway fresh vegetable section, which he thought was pretty funny. He explained some very interesting things about farm technology and genetic crop modification. I assumed that he'd gone bust out there on the windy flats and that was why he was working as a handyman at the gym. Later, someone told me that Augie was a millionaire and had written a seminal book on high-plains groundcover technology. He just liked being around all the friendly people at the gym.

Things like this never happened to me before I got sober in AA. In the past, I was only interested in people or information that could be of use to me. I knew I wouldn't need the information Augie was giving me, but I liked hearing it and I liked getting to know him. Just for the record, I'm not having a flashback to the generational solidarity of the late 1960s, nor am I under the spell of some notion of world peace through friendliness. But I recognize that cold-hearted self-ishness was part of what made me miserable as a drinker and that a smile and a friendly word are not too much to contribute to the better world I live in today. However, I'm too old to wave a lighter around at rock concerts.

AA Relationships

Let me add a final word on the subject of relationships in AA. Not every reader has a frame of reference for this, and some of you will simply not care. But AAs are a completely new category of friends for me, and I want to tell you about them.

After I got out of rehab and started participating in meetings, I was amazed at how perceptive, interesting, and wise people had gotten while I was out drunk. Of course, not everyone is brilliant or profound. Not everyone tells me something I need to know right now. Not everyone gets to the point fast enough for me, but then sometimes I don't know what the point really is. Even people with poor grammar and those who pepper every sentence with the word "like" seem to have something to say to me these days. I have to watch out for my tendency to patronize, but just listening and bringing a little tolerance to bear have led me to some very worthwhile people that I would otherwise never have met. Let me give you an example.

I had been seeing Riley in AA meetings around town for almost a year. He was a very scary, big guy with a deep voice, although he hardly ever talked. I knew he was dangerous because he broke a window at one meeting. Once, when he was asked to read the AA preamble, he tore it up and told the chairman to go screw himself. After a few months, I noticed that Riley had begun staring at me during meetings and I knew I had to confront him somehow. I began toasting him with my coffee cup and boldly saying, "What's up, Riley?" Of course, I didn't have the least interest in what was up with Riley and could only imagine what a depraved landscape that probably was.

One day I was sitting in a meeting and another AA came over to me and whispered, "Riley's outside and he wants to see you." I didn't like hearing that. As I sauntered outside, I told myself that I could always scream if I had to. I sized him up as I walked toward him. He looked crazy, but he always did. He was smoking, so that meant he probably wasn't preparing to assault me. I decided to take control of the conversation. I toasted him with my coffee cup and said, "What's up, Riley?" He burst into tears. I was flabbergasted.

He talked to me in his maddeningly halting manner (which suddenly seemed only sincere), and I just listened. His immediate problem was that he had quit his construction job that morning. This was the only noncriminal job he had ever held. Crime paid well, and when he came into AA, Riley owned two houses. He gave them both to homeless men. He told me that he didn't come into AA to recover but to find "a peaceful place to die." He had torn up the AA preamble at that meeting because he never learned to read.

When he finally took a breath, I asked, "Why me, Riley?" He said that I was a "big part" of his recovery, which came as astonishing news to me. We entered AA at about the same time, and Riley believed that as long as I stayed sober and the program seemed to be working in my life, it could work in his too. We talked for another fifteen minutes or so, and I invited Riley to call me later that night if he wanted to.

He did, and I found out that he was a reasonably bright guy who had never really caught a break in life before AA. The next day, I gave him some job tips and he gave me a key chain with the Serenity Prayer on it. Riley and I are now a lot more relaxed with one another, and I genuinely enjoy his company at AA meetings. We're not fishing buddies, but maybe that's because I don't fish. I don't feel sorry for Riley at all. He's a survivor. I accept him and he accepts me, and that's a good thing for both of us. Before AA, I could never have made this kind of connection with a person so different from me—and that would have been my loss.

On the whole, I've found that AA people are pretty likeable. We're fairly open-minded and don't judge others indiscriminately. We're interested in others but know how to mind our own business. Some of the funniest people in America are in AA, although AA humor may seem a little dark. I think that AAs have above-average IQs, despite repeated, toxic attacks on our own brains. AAs are achievers and typically industrious. It's true that some AAs can go overboard on the spirituality business, but you won't see anyone suiting up in a saffron robe before a meeting. The focus for most of us remains on the tangible results of our programs in our everyday lives.

Maybe what attracts me most to AAs is that they seem to be able to get to the point of trust faster than average people, and they intuitively know that solid relationships are built on actions, not words or intentions. Trust and action are central to the AA program, so it's no surprise that many of us end up rebuilding our personal lives from that brick and mortar.

AA relationships are exactly like "normal" relationships except where they're different. I've made some great friends in AA and will do business with an AA if I can, before going to the Yellow Pages. I've lent smallish amounts of money to AAs who are down on their luck with no expectation of being paid back (and often I'm not). I've seen AAs work substantial business deals among themselves on the basis of assumed integrity. From underwriter to undertaker, I'll usually choose an AA. I hasten to add that AAs are not snow white, especially when we first come in. For example, newer members are probably not the best pick for trustee or CFO at your company. But that's more about common sense than AA.

I've seen a number of AA marriages; in fact, there are two great ones in my own extended family. There may be some risk in committing to a person who's taken so many wrong turns in life. On the other hand, you get some extra wisdom and tolerance in the bargain. If having things in common is a good predictor of success in marriage, AA marriages are common background on steroids. Not all AA marriages work but a lot of them do, and teaming up with another member can be an excellent option if you remember the one-year rule (see "Thirteenth-Stepping" on page 140).

I said AA relationships are different, and the difference is this. We are AAs in the first place because we share a mortal affliction. All the goodness in AA notwithstanding, ours is a fellowship of people who hold despair and death at bay. Even in our lightest moments together, there's something

I call the "Lazarus Effect." ("Geez, Lazarus, I thought you were dead! You look good! How do you feel?") We can never forget that we came to AA as condemned men and women, that we enjoy only a daily reprieve from alcoholism, and that we will never walk away cured. As grim as that may sound, it looks like a very good deal to most of us.

Afterword

"It just keeps getting better and better and better. It really does."

—Ray Bob S., AA member since 1954

I picked one year as the time frame for this book because I was pretty sure when I started to write that I would have my A-game back by the end of my first year. At six months, I was feeling great—AA was making sense and steadily delivering results that I could see. By the nine-month mark I felt as though I had fully recovered physically and my mental acuity was sharper than I could remember it being in some time. I was on a spiritual path to somewhere good. By my own measure, I was ahead of schedule.

But then something funny happened . . . or did not happen. I didn't plateau off as I assumed I eventually would. I kept making progress in all three areas of my recovery: body, mind, and spirit. As I write this at the one-year anniversary of my last drink, I've come to accept a radical notion. Permanent progress in my sobriety and in the quality of my life *is* my A-game now. I was pretty amazed when this started to sink in. I asked around, and many other AAs told me that the same thing was happening for them. Not all, of course. Some AAs seem to have more than their fair share of detours and struggles, and some just do not seem to make it at all. However, I am absolutely convinced that if we keep working the program, better things just keep happening for most of us.

It was around this time that I experienced another moment of clarity about AA. If I could make a go of it, surely many others could too. All I had really done was to turn my despair into motivation and my selfishness into action. The rest was about showing up. This may be an oversimplification, but complexity is a dangerous thicket for us alcoholics. We can hide in it and we can get lost in it. Every time I tried to analyze AA, I risked missing something important, like making progress or seeing results. My principal motivation in writing this book is not to decode AA. It's to try to get more suffering alcoholics through the door of an AA meeting or two.

At one of my early meetings, I heard someone say that the beauty of coming into AA is that we "never have to take another drink if we don't want to." That had a powerful effect on me, and it turned out to be true. AA is not a collection of glum, defeated losers. It's a fellowship of happy, confident survivors. Getting there is not as hard as you might think— and what are you doing for the next year that's more important, anyway?

My friend Ray Bob is right: our AA life keeps getting better and better and better. All we have to do is go to a meeting and keep coming back. If we work at it, we get to live undrunk.

The Twelve Steps of Alcoholics Anonymous*

1. We admitted we were powerless over alcohol—that our lives had become unmanageable.

2. Came to believe that a Power greater than ourselves could restore us to sanity.

3. Made a decision to turn our will and our lives over to the care of God *as we understood Him.*

4. Made a searching and fearless moral inventory of ourselves.

5. Admitted to God, to ourselves, and to another human being the exact nature of our wrongs.

6. Were entirely ready to have God remove all these defects of character.

7. Humbly asked Him to remove our shortcomings.

8. Made a list of all persons we had harmed, and became willing to make amends to them all.

9. Made direct amends to such people wherever possible, except when to do so would injure them or others.

10. Continued to take personal inventory and when we were wrong promptly admitted it.

---

* The Twelve Steps of Alcoholics Anonymous are reprinted from *Alcoholics Anonymous,* 4th ed. (New York: AA World Services, Inc., 2001), 59–60.

11. Sought through prayer and meditation to improve our conscious contact with God *as we understood Him,* praying only for knowledge of His will for us and the power to carry that out.

12. Having had a spiritual awakening as the result of these steps, we tried to carry this message to alcoholics, and to practice these principles in all our affairs.

Some Recommended Readings

There are many AAs who believe that *Alcoholics Anonymous* is all we need to read to fully understand the fellowship and benefit from the program. That's true. The Big Book is a remarkably comprehensive and enduring text. No one I've met in AA thinks it needs a twenty-first-century edit or something like a New Testament sequel. It stands on its own, it's user friendly, and it works.

But I'm a reader, so over the past year, I ended up with my nose in a fairly wide selection of books about alcoholism in general and AA in particular. I wanted some added perspective on the Big Book from psychology, philosophy, theology, sociology, and medicine. Of the books I read this year, the following four illuminated some facet of AA that ended up being especially important to me.

The Varieties of Religious Experience by William James was first published in 1902. This collection of twenty lectures given at the University of Edinburgh has been called "the most important work on religion produced in America." William D. Silkworth, M.D., gave Bill Wilson a copy in 1934, while Bill was in Towns Hospital undergoing what would be his last treatment for alcoholism. Some of the most important concepts in the Big Book, including surrender and spiritual experience, probably came to Bill from *Varieties*.

Modern Man in Search of a Soul (1933), by Carl Gustav Jung helps set Jung apart from his contemporary Sigmund Freud, and it is a readable exposition of Jung's thinking about the psychology of religion. It's unclear whether Bill Wilson read this book, but he publicly acknowledged the influence on AA of Jung's conception of the role of spirituality in mental health. Bill referred to the Swiss psychiatrist as an AA "founder," by which he probably meant something like intellectual inspiration. Wilson and Jung finally corresponded directly shortly before the latter's death in 1961.

A Joseph Campbell Companion (1991), edited by Campbell disciple Diane K. Osbon. Longtime Sarah Lawrence professor and Esalen Institute guru, Campbell was importantly influenced by Jung. He wrote eloquently about spiritualism and what he saw as a set of universal concepts and truths that link religions across time and around the world. For AAs struggling to reconcile myth, religion, and spirituality, Campbell's brush is a broad one. I have a friend who embraced Taoism some years ago in support of his AA program. He credits Campbell with helping him find a spiritual life when nothing else seemed to click.

Beyond the Influence (2000), by Katherine Ketcham and William F. Asbury, is a layman-friendly review of thinking on alcoholism in the medical and treatment communities. The science of understanding and treating alcoholism has come a long way since Bill and Bob and their fellow "dipsomaniacs" got together in the 1930s to try to figure themselves out. I felt a need to understand something about the emerging science, and *Beyond the Influence* was the ticket.

More Tried-and-True Core Recovery Books

Living Sober. New York: AA World Services, Inc., 1998.

Daily Reflections. New York: AA World Services, Inc., 1990.

Twenty-Four Hours a Day. Center City, MN: Hazelden, 1992.

Alcoholics Anonymous. 4th ed. New York: AA World Services, Inc., 2001.

B., Mel. *Walk in Dry Places.* Center City, MN: Hazelden, 1996.

About the Author

A. J. Adams, a recovering alcoholic, consults, writes, and teaches. He lives with his wife in the Southwest. A. J. Adams is a pen name.